"Rich with his own experience and straightforward talk, Robert Rabbin pulls no punches as he addresses the core qualities for being a responsible person in today's highly complex, fast-moving world. It's refreshing to read such a clear prescription for returning to our essence as human beings. After all, our world will only change after we change ourselves. This book is an absolute must for anyone who claims to want change to happen."

—**Anita Roddick, founder and co-chair of The Body Shop International**

"It's raw, original, organic, clear, unashamed, deeply spiritual and direct. It's the breakthrough book we've been waiting for."

—**Martin Rutte, president, Livelihood; co-author of *Chicken Soup for the Soul at Work***

"Hallelujah! Joy, joy, joy. At last someone has had the courage to take a revolutionary stance in favor of psychic and spiritual liberation. No longer can spirituality be confined to the ashram, the forest, or the house of prayer. Robert Rabbin is passionate and eloquent in his declaration that, from this moment forth, only mystics—true mystics—can be viewed as qualified leaders and decision-makers. Any lesser standard is simply too foolhardy and reckless. I wholeheartedly support and endorse his enthusiasm. His is the voice of wisdom. Robert Rabbin is calling for a liberation of the human soul. My greatest wish is that his call will be heard and heeded in the boardrooms and offices of every corporation. The time has come to shake off the chains of materialism and unconscious habit that have held us the prisoners of our own minds."

—**Jeffrey Mishlove, Ph. D., president of the Intuition Network, author of *The PK Man*, and host of the national public television series "Thinking Allowed"**

Igniting
the Soul
at Work

A Mandate for Mystics

Robert Rabbin

HAMPTON ROADS
PUBLISHING COMPANY, INC.

This book is a revised edition of
Invisible Leadership: Igniting the Soul.

Cover design by Steve Amarillo

Hampton Roads Publishing Company, Inc.
1125 Stoney Ridge Road
Charlottesville, VA 22902

434-296-2772
fax: 434-296-5096
e-mail: hrpc@hrpub.com
www.hrpub.com

If you are unable to order this book from your local
bookseller, you may order directly from the publisher.
Call 1-800-766-8009, toll-free.
Library of Congress Catalog Card Number:2002103102
ISBN 1-57174-271-9
10 9 8 7 6 5 4 3 2 1
Printed on acid-free paper in Canada

Credits

Grateful acknowledgment is made for permission to use copyrighted material:

Forsyth, Karl, "Television Robs Our Children of Their Potential," Computers in Education web site (http://www.corecom.net/~karlfpp/asd-comp.htm).

Havel, Václav, "The Need for Transcendence in the Postmodern World," Independence Hall, Philadelphia, Pa, 1994, Václav Havel web site (http://www.hrad.cz/president/Havel/speeches/index_uk.html).

Mitchell, Jennifer D., "Editorial: The Tigers," *World•Watch,* Washington, D.C., Vol. 11, No. 1, January/February 1998.

Robbins, Tom, "The Meaning of Life," Special Supplement Insert, *Life Magazine,* Vol. 14, No. 16, December 1991.

Acknowledgments

With gratitude to

Sandra
sister of the century

Deborah
the dearest of friends

Arline
may she experience profound peace

Leo and Anna
my dear ones of the desert

Leah Grillo
my good friend and art teacher,
and the world's greatest soccer player

Contents

Introduction

I recently heard film director Sydney Pollack tell the story of how he struggled to find the "spine" of the movie *Tootsie,* which he directed. He said it was crucial to know any movie's spine—its essence—which involves asking and answering several core questions: What is this movie really about? What is its meaning? What is the story it wants to tell? What is the impact it wants to have? Once the movie's spine is clearly articulated, Pollack said, you can move forward with a certain sense of assurance, relating all the elements of the movie to that central spine, the core purpose of the movie.

This book has a spine too. In fact, it has two spines. The first spine, the one which took possession of me in the beginning and taught me about the second spine as I wrote, cannot be clearly articulated. I cannot say what it is. I don't mean it's a secret or that I don't want to tell you. It literally cannot be said. No one—not poet, artist, saint, sage, shaman, mystic, or philosopher—has ever been able to speak about the first spine of this book, an experience which defies description and explanation.

If you were holding a gun to my head, forcing me to say something, I would say the first spine of this book is *silence,* though even that flawless word only orbits the truth. Silence, wonder, awe, union, grace—we can only stutter approximations of those moments in which we become possessed by something greater than ourselves, which at the same time is our most authentic self. We have all had encounters with this mysterious, yet stupendously real, dimension of living in which we recognize universal truths about ourselves, reality, and the meaning and purpose of life.

Possessed by silence during the writing of this book, I watched the second spine take shape and form as though watching a movie unfold before me. The second spine of this book is about awareness, reality, and a true life—an authentic life of passion, pulse, and power; the kind of life which we enjoy during feasts of silence, the life of our greatest longing, the life of freedom, joy, and courage, the life that thrills us and others with its sheer power, clarity, and majesty. It is about that life which is bestowed upon us by the very hand of God as we are lifted and transported to Olympian mountain peaks, there to dance and sing our secret songs of life and love.

We have all danced on mountain peaks. Whether we know and remember or not, whether for the merest of moments or for eternities, we have all danced on mountain peaks. And when we dance on mountain peaks in our pristine primordial glory of being, we dance with the first spine of this book: silence.

Perhaps we cannot stay forever in the rarefied atmosphere of those peaks. Perhaps we must come down to live again in the valleys and plains of more common days and nights. But we must not leave the silent spine and soul of our mountaintop dancing. We must take these with us to the ground below and to our lives in the more mortal world of day-to-day responsibilities. As we descend, we are likely to forget. We must not.

Rene Daumal wrote in *Mount Analogue,* "You cannot stay on the summit forever; you have to come down again. So why bother in the first place? Just this: what is above knows what is below, but what is below does not know what is above. One climbs, one sees. One descends, one sees no longer but one has seen. There is an art to conducting oneself in the lower regions by the memory of what one saw higher up. When one can no longer see, one can at least still know."

This book is about living that mountaintop knowing in the midst of our flat and often forgetful world. Within this knowing, within this heightened beauty, meaning, and significance, our soul ignites with recognition, our flailing minds stop and tilt—and in that tilt of our usual mind the spectacular order and intelligence of reality emerges. Awakening to reality is to step out of self, time, and place where we are met by eternity and tutored. Then we can return home to family and friends and practice the lessons learned in the primordial silence.

There is one last thing I want to mention, a kind of disclaimer. I am not interested in appealing to anyone's rational mind, to inform or persuade, to explain or define. Explanations will not take us far enough, and definitions are insufficient tools for the work before us. I hear the poet Kabir shout in my left ear, "Those who hope to be reasonable about it fail. The arrogance of reason has separated us from that love."

One does not come to insight and wisdom through reason, which can only persuade or convince, not intoxicate. Our reasoning cannot reach silence or touch the soul; it can only grease the gears and pulleys of the mind.

The soul needs another lubricant; the soul needs to feed—no, to feast—on inspiration. Gorging on inspiration, the soul explodes in love. To know what must be known about ourselves, we must catapult from all that is reasonable so as to know that inspiration is practical, self-knowledge is relevant, and love is essential.

I hope this book will take us away from the safe shores of reason and convention. I am after bigger fish than intellectual comprehension, agreement or disagreement. I want to push out into a reckless sea and risk comfort for the sake of that which is beyond the mind and intellect. I seek to evoke your wild heart of ecstatic love, for it is this heart and its knowing that we need to embrace.

Let us take note that Jelaluddin Rumi, the 13th century Persian mystic, is the best-selling poet in America. He is frequently quoted by speakers, authors, consultants, and teachers as representing a rare and penetrating wisdom. If we are going to let him speak for us, should we not honor his words with our actions? Should we not take to the floor, as he would, and begin our slow and meticulous dance toward the center of ecstatic love?

The clock has struck the crucial hour. It is morning now, and time to wake up, time for all of us to get dressed and go to work touching this world with the transcendent flame of our fully lit souls. Let us each be responsible for this. Let us each be a leader in a radical social rebellion of torching the world where we work with our blazing souls.

This is the mystics' mandate: lead the world into peace with your fully lit soul.

1

Transcendent Leadership

The vocabulary of spiritual awakening and transformation has entered the mainstream of society and has penetrated the hearts and minds of a growing number of avant-garde leaders. Corporate America is flirting with innovative paradigms that emphasize moral and ethical values, as well as social and environmental responsibility. Visionary leaders are endowing organizations with principles and values born of spiritual awakening. Words like spirit, soul, enlightenment, and sacred are as apt to be spoken in traditional bunkers of conservative capitalism as they are in spiritual communities and subcultures.

As leaders seek to cure social ills, as executives seek to energize and humanize the workplace, as individuals seek to live out their deepest values, new dialogues are taking place about the nature, purpose, and function of leadership. I would like to enter that dialogue with a radical agenda, a revolutionary notion just barely visible on the screen of public discourse. The premise of this agenda is the assertion that the transcendent, mystical experience of unitive consciousness is a prerequisite for effective leadership. Transcendent awareness is the yeast that leavens all other leadership skills, abilities, and agendas.

The external world is a direct expression of our internal world of thoughts, ideas, and beliefs. In order to transform society, we must first transform ourselves. We must each first investigate our own hearts and minds; we must each discover how we create and project the very things we want to change in the world. The power of transcendent awareness will, in and of itself, transform our lives, institutions, organizations, and society at large. This direct experience of our spiritual center—of our inherent spiritual consciousness, free from distortions and conditioning—will show us how to live and work in a sacred and meaningful way.

Much will be asked of leaders in the coming years. They will be expected to help redress an array of social problems, to help cure illness, end epidemics, feed the hungry, end brutality and war, stop the displacement of indigenous tribes, reverse the pollution and degradation of the environment, curtail corruption and greed, safely dispose of industrial and nuclear waste, and educate children without crushing their free and spiritual minds. These problems are solvable by us—all of us, together, each contributing in a unique way—if we sincerely want to and if we will use the preeminent power of our inherent transcendent awareness.

I believe that awareness is more useful and practical than intellectual strategies, models, principles, answers, and prescriptions: I believe our own dormant powers of pure awareness can reveal instantly what we must do and how we must do it. To explore our consciousness and expand our awareness of reality is to climb high enough to see the whole landscape of cause and effect. We have betrayed ourselves by turning from the light of transcendent awareness. We have become entranced by the visible world and have forgotten its invisible, immaterial origins within consciousness. We have fallen in love with the arguments of our mind and forgotten the profound counsel of our soul. We have become belligerent toward nature and our carelessness is starting to pile up like stinking garbage. We are willing to do almost anything for money, and we are silent witnesses to the desecration of entire populations. I know this is not the whole story, but it is a part of the story that is important to consider in light of our capacity for mystical knowledge. We need to discover our own inner capacity for mystical knowledge in order to bring balance and sanity to an otherwise fractured life. In this alliance with reality, each of us will be able to apply unprecedented invention and wisdom to those diseases of our lives; we will become gift and grace bestowing behemoths; we will restore the lost paradise for ourselves, for each other, and for the entire living Earth—and future generations will revere us for our great effort and work.

This book is my contribution to the public discourse about who we are, where we are going, and how we are going to get there. I believe in the power of the awakened soul and its clear, undivided awareness. I believe that we are all linked to the mystical source of creation, and waking up to that fact is not as difficult as it may seem. I believe that we'll be fine if we simply drive our tent poles deep into the earth of that essential ground and stay put. After that, let whatever comes, come. Let whatever is to happen, happen. We'll be ready.

Once we are standing knee deep in the radiant earth of our soul, I trust absolutely and beyond any doubt in our collective spirit and ingenuity to create new values; and from those new values, new priorities and commitments; and from those, new systems, structures, and institutions. I know that we can transform fear into freedom, hatred into love, violence into peace, poverty into abundance, pollution into purity, and separation into connection.

We have only this one thing to do, only this one thing: show the face of who we truly are, that we and others may see the brilliance of that true face and know its redemptive love and wisdom. If we want to know how to do this, how to find and show the brilliant face of our inner truth, the answer is this: *want to.* We must simply *want* this more than anything else. That is all. Put nothing else in front of this one desire, and your face will burst like a thousand suns upon this newly-happy Earth.

It is my hope that something in this book—a word, a phrase, a story—will cause your world to stop, your mind to tilt, and your soul to ignite in silence. I believe that the soul, fully aroused and on fire, irreversibly awake, is the greatest power in the world. If we can hear our soul's silence as loudly as the silence of the high desert at night, then we will know exactly how to bring ourselves and the world of our making into accord with reality—and we will do it with wisdom and love.

For Personal Reflection

Write down your initial reactions to this first chapter. Don't censor your thoughts. Let your thoughts flow easily and effortlessly onto the page. Keep writing until your hand slows. Read what you have written. Will you now consider putting all those thoughts and reactions to the side and out of your mind? Will you consider reading the rest of this book with an open mind, free of the beliefs that your first exercise has revealed?

2

Leading from Within

In the Dalai Lama's acceptance speech for the Nobel Peace Prize a few years ago, he said, "Because we all share this small planet Earth, we have to learn to live in harmony and peace with each other and with nature. That is not just a dream, but a necessity."

This is an important scouting report from the frontier of consciousness. It is so simple, and yet so critical. "To live in harmony and peace with each other and with nature" is the first job of leadership, its top priority and goal.

Wherever we are, we must begin now to live in harmony and peace with each other and with nature. We've got to honestly evaluate our motives and actions to see if they are in accord with life, in harmony and peace with each other, and with nature. Are we, or are we not, truly and deeply committed to harmony and peace with each other and with nature? If we are not, then we must change. If we are, then let's get on with it. This is a firm line in the sand. It is a nonnegotiable requirement of leadership. There is no middle ground, no political gamesmanship, and no public relations spinning double talk that can compromise this.

If we are to establish a new planetary order, we must first establish an equivalent order within ourselves, which can then serve as the foundation for a new order of purpose, values, and ethics in our world. If we are to transform ourselves, and thus the world, we must discover some basic truths about who we are. We must begin to question our ideas and beliefs, not just defend them even as we attack others'. Obviously, we must do this because our old ideas and beliefs have not led us to live in peace and harmony with each other, and certainly not with nature.

We have to travel into the deep interior of our inner consciousness and explore its riches for transformative insights. I think we must go here, into the silence, to find out how we can create a new order. In this silence we will discover the designs needed to realize peace and harmony. In this silence we encounter our unity, and in unity we experience peace. This awareness is universal, it is timeless, and it is supremely significant. Within this crucible of silence, transcendent leaders are forged.

For Personal Reflection

Imagine that you are the Dalai Lama's speech writer. Imagine that he has asked you to write a four-minute talk, using his words at the beginning of this chapter as the main point he wants to get across. Write this talk, and then give it to a small group of family, friends, or colleagues.

3

Mandate for Mystics

I want to completely redefine the word "leader" to imply a person's attainments in the realm of consciousness so that from now on, direct experience with reality is a prerequisite for leadership. "Leader" and "mystic" should be synonymous. A mystic is a person who has direct and immediate experience of reality. A mystic's knowledge is not based on religious ideologies, creeds, or beliefs; it comes spontaneously as one merges into life itself.

Though spirituality and mysticism are gaining some acceptance within our culture, our society as a whole is still suspicious of spirituality and tends to marginalize mystics as a fringe element. We have forgotten that every religion was founded by a mystic, and that the heart of the world's spiritual traditions is the mystical experience. While we may allow the words of long-dead mystics to console and uplift our spirits and broken souls, we are not yet inclined to allow their radical views to mold the ways and means of our commerce and social conduct. We seem to believe that their visions and words are not practical enough to guide and sustain us in our mundane pursuits.

If real-life mystics happen to enter today's marketplace, we don't allow their views to inform and shape our decision making in the "real" world of business, government, and education; we certainly wouldn't trust a mystic in the role of a general or admiral, or as CEO of Bank of America. Mystics just cannot produce results in the material world; they don't understand how the world works. It's best if mystics stay in the ghettos of spirituality, where we can visit if and when we want. This is the common wisdom, which is not wisdom at all, but pure foolishness.

Part of this misperception about the competency of mystics is due to the nature of the mystic's path. As mystics are weaned, by meditation and silence, from their addiction to materialism, they naturally lose interest in the physical, visible world in order to more fully explore and appreciate the truer and more encompassing immaterial, invisible world of spirit. This is analogous to a medical intern forsaking, for a time, all life except for the life within the confines of a hospital. It is analogous to anyone who wants to achieve greatness and proficiency in an art or science. There is a time when they must devote themselves single-mindedly and exclusively to their chosen field. I'm sure that Baryshnikov, when he was young, didn't just take a couple of dance lessons. Mystics intern in reality and study consciousness and awareness. Until they reach a level of maturity, they may not retain a strong relationship to the material world, mistakenly called the "real" world. However, when mystics achieve a certain level of maturity, of proficiency in their art, they may be returned by silence to this physical world with a clarity of vision and a dexterity of action whose purpose is to awaken, inspire, teach, and lead others to their own deep truth. Some of these mystics are beginning to be seen and heard outside the ghettos of spiritual communities.

The prevailing conventional view that mysticism is disconnected from the real world is dead wrong. It is an unfortunate hallucination. The mystic path reveals reality. The premise of this book is to show that unless and until people embark on a mystical path of knowledge, they are delusional, and represent a real and present danger to themselves and to others. The central truth of this book is that if we are not actively and vigorously exploring and expanding our awareness, then we are not qualified for leadership of any kind. At this time, with so much on the line, we simply must have leaders who can end madness by the sheer power of their clarity of cause and effect, their empathy toward reality, and their resoluteness to live and work as servants of life itself.

I am proposing that from now on, we—as a people, as a culture—allow and accept only mystics, mature mystics who hold in one hand the invisible world and in the other hand the visible, to have decision making authority in our society. These individuals will be an entirely new species of leader who will serve us by serving the creative power of the universe and the mystic oneness from which all life comes. Their role, their job definition, is to know this power, to align with this power, to be taken, and finally to merge with this power. These leaders, these mature and maturing mystics, do not live in ashrams and convents, in monasteries and on mountaintops. They live here, where you live; they work right here, where you work. They stand squarely on asphalt and Astroturf; in bowling alleys, shopping malls, airports, and boardrooms, with cell phones and pagers. These leaders drive in the carpool lanes every morning at 6:00 a.m. in Chevrolets, BMWs, and 4x4s. But they are driving in an ocean of clarity, setting everything in order by serving reality.

Our society is reality challenged, and this handicap has created problems, sadness, and suffering. We are *koyaanisqatsi,* a Hopi word which means "crazy life, life in turmoil, life disintegrating, life out of balance, a state of life that calls for another way of living." Our society is koyaanisqatsi. You know it and I know it.

We can correct the imbalance through a radical shift in our consciousness. We do not lack money, know-how, time, or resources. We lack only awareness, and even this we do not really lack, but only forget to use. We'll have to get to work and refurbish our awareness with paint, furniture, and light fixtures made of reality, throwing out everything that is made of egoistic delusions. I am suggesting that we need to see the world as our painting, and that we must begin to paint with a mystic's eye, with a lover's brush, and a palette of colors shocking to the conventional mind. We need a revolution of consciousness.

The mystic's canvas is a transcendent one, painted in the time beyond timelessness, where truth can never be spoken but is as real as concrete, finch, fire truck, or sea urchins basking in the early morning tide pools. The mystic's art transcends the pettiness and misperceptions of doctrines and beliefs; the mystic's art depicts our world and other worlds, our bodies and interstellar space, boardrooms and lucid dreams, glaciers and insects. The mystic's artful eye is opened wide and beholds the love-pulse within all living creatures; the mystic paints this in sudden downpours of color and intuition, of insight and primal sounds. Mystics square dance with supernovas on Friday nights. They live as the servants of life's love-pulse and so happily and humbly serve each living thing. Their only purpose is to know and serve reality, to ignite the spiritual passion and intensity of everyone they meet.

For Personal Reflection

Are you currently involved in activities or practices intended to expand your awareness of yourself and the nature of reality? Do you feel that such activities should be kept separate from work? If so, why? If not, how do these activities influence your conduct in the workplace?

4

The "S" Word: Soul

Whenever I use the word "soul" in talks to business audiences, someone invariably asks, "What do you mean by soul?" Even though I said earlier I wanted to evoke, not explain or define, this is an honest and sincere question which deserves a respectful answer.

If we're going to use the word "soul" in the context of leadership and business, we'd better define it, we'd better understand its meaning clearly. Otherwise, this single word—so often thought of as abstract, esoteric, and impractical—will probably create much confusion, doubt, and maybe even cynicism. Let me tell you what I mean by soul, and how I think it relates to our work lives in very practical and useful ways.

There are many definitions of soul, some more precise than others, according to various religious, spiritual, and metaphysical belief systems, varying from culture to culture. I use the words "spirit" and "soul" in the same way, meaning the vital principle or animating force within living beings. These words refer to a dimension of living which opens before us from time to time with such compelling force that we fall to our knees in silence, awe, and gratitude. Soul refers to those gorgeous moments of self-transcendence, of love, of joy, and communion with the whole of existence in which our seeing becomes acute and our knowing becomes wise. I use the word "soul" as a poetic image that refers to a life of significant meaning born of deep inner exploration.

When these disruptions to our conventional way of living occur, it's as though we see another dimension of life about which we were ignorant. The mask of appearance falls away, and we see something profound about life. We experience something that is timeless. It's beyond words, and the mind hardly grasps it. In these moments, the fortifications against the soul dissolve and a new perspective appears.

Let's go into this a bit deeper and see what this soul perspective implies for us. From this perspective and in this remembrance, what do we know about what I am calling the soul and its importance to our work lives?

Soul implies a real and living connection to others. Recognizing this connection with others means that we must treat others with respect, kindness, compassion, and dignity. Who would not like to be treated in this manner?

Soul implies beauty. This means that our actions must preserve the natural beauty of life in all its manifestations. Recognizing the natural beauty of life, we will not destroy, pollute, defile, or degrade anything. This is a sound principle to guide us in our business decisions, is it not?

Soul implies truth. This means we must speak the truth, we must be accountable for our actions, and we must be straightforward in our dealings with each other and with the communities of which we are a part. Recognizing this, we are bound to honesty and full disclosure of our actions. This would be a refreshing stance for business leaders to take, don't you think?

Soul implies balance and harmony. This means we must keep our priorities in order and give equal time to our own personal growth, to our families, to our communities—to those pursuits and activities that enrich our whole life. Recognizing the need for balance, we will not be compulsive or greedy, we will not sacrifice the integrity of this moment for a future promise. This will keep us sane, healthy, and energetic.

Soul implies universality. This means that we are all shareholders in certain basic values. What do we all want? We all want to be appreciated, to be accepted, to make a positive contribution to others. We want to feel that our lives and our labors make a positive difference. We want to give, to serve, to be the reason for someone else's happiness and well-being. I would like to think that we all are servants of other people's happiness.

Soul implies inspiration and deep passion. This means that we live and work from our hearts, from what we truly love. If we follow our hearts to work, we will not need to be motivated by some cheap management trick to give our best effort. Our heart will always ask us to give our best, for the sake of love and passion. We will not need to be bribed. Enthusiasm, cooperation, and commitment are the hallmarks of a heartfelt life. Is there anything we could not accomplish, together, working from and with our hearts?

Soul implies joy. This means that we work from joy, with joy, and toward joy. This is not a Pollyanna principle, because I think that everything we do in life is for the sake of joy. Let's be honest about it: no one likes to work in an environment of tedium, depression, and sadness. Let joy be our standard: if joy is present, we are doing things right, and doing things well. If not, we are doing things wrong, and we should stop and figure out how to get back on track.

Soul implies going beyond conventional boundaries. This means we should always feel free to risk new ideas, new approaches to old problems. This means we should develop our minds, bodies, and spirits so that they shine with creativity and innovation. Recognizing this, we welcome boldness, diversity, and initiative. We should be open to continuous learning and growth, not just in business strategies, but in living. I hope that we are all growing in self-awareness each day.

Soul implies clarity and awareness. This means that we speak and act consciously and conscientiously. Being conscious means being aware of those impulses, motives, and intentions that drive us. Conscious awareness is the moment-to-moment clarity of motive and intent. It is a balanced alignment among thought, word, and action. Awareness means to be deeply in touch with our thoughts and emotions every moment. Awareness means that we are able to see what is actually happening around us, and not just our own projected fantasies and ideas of what is happening. Being conscious is a commitment to an ongoing process of self-inquiry and discovery, of illuminating those unlit aspects of our subconscious that often drive us without our knowing.

This is what I mean by "soul" at work. I do not presume to be the authority on this; I do not want you to think I am laying down an exact formula. But if we continue this line of inquiry in our respective work-places, I believe we will open up great and wonderful possibilities. I believe any organization that encourages such a dialogue will stand at the very forefront of meaningful change and progress. I believe that such organizations will be known as much for what they do as for how they do it; such organizations will be known as much for their products and services as for their ethics, values, and principles.

Liberating and nourishing the human soul within the workplace is a gift the world sorely needs at this time. Please be generous in your giving.

For Personal Reflection

What is your definition of "soul"? Is this definition based on what others have told you, on what you have read, or on your own direct experience? Does your awareness of soul guide your choices and decisions in life? Have you ever had a conversation about soul with colleagues in the workplace?

5

We Are All Mystics

I was born in 1950 and had my first spiritual experience eleven years later, when the hand that made this world reached into my bedroom window and shook me awake. I had been skiing with my family at Sestrierre, near our home in Torino, Italy, when I fell on the slopes and broke my left leg in three places. In a cast up to my hip, I spent a month in bed. During that time, I started leafing through the *World Book Encyclopedia*. I remember my amazement as I wandered through many worlds, turning page after page. Reading about the universe, its origins and vastness was a powerful initiation into mystery and awe. I sensed that behind this visible world is an invisible world, a world of spirit, a world too subtle for my senses to see and touch, but real nonetheless.

One day, I felt a presence enter the room. I could feel it but not see it; even so, my eyes widened. I became silent and attentive. Then I just *knew*. This presence is the conscious, creative power of the spiritual world. This presence is God. I am this presence. So are you.

Anyone who knows this presence is a mystic. Mysticism refers to this presence, to the unfathomable mystery of creation. I know that tomes have been written on the subjects of God, mysticism, soul, mind, and reality, some of which require lifetimes of study. It is a vast field, with innumerable nuances of meaning and truth. There is much scholarly debate about the difference between real spiritual experience and hallucination, between the first level and third level spiritual experience, whether a vision of the blue pearl is higher than the green pearl, or if there are seven chakras or thirteen. Some people clamor for scientific proof of a spiritual experience.

I am not interested in models of mysticism or theories of spiritual evolution. The study of spirituality is very different from direct experience—the province of mystics. To explain mysticism is very different from demonstrating it. The spiritual world of the mystic is a wild sea, one which we long to enter. Once we enter it, it won't let go of us, and we'll continue to learn more and more. But let's just get our feet wet to begin with.

A mystic is simply a person who has experienced the heart of life, and who thus knows that an essence—love, truth, spirit, silence, self, consciousness, Tao, God—exists everywhere, pervading everything. I believe that we are all mystics because we have all been deeply touched and moved by an epiphany or struck by splendor in a sumptuous lightning flash that lifts body, mind, and heart into the soul of the world's creative power. In this collision with essence, we stretch ourselves from here and now to places and times both past and future; we become part of the endless inscrutability of life itself. Mystics see their lives in that instant as a gift and function of a universal force of consciousness, and in that same moment become drenched with clarity, love, wisdom, and compassion, which are the inescapable fragrances of the spiritual life. Seeing life in this way, one's mind and spirit become free, inventive, and generous; one sees oneself everywhere. We live within a mystical nexus with life, with spirit, with God.

A mystic learns to live in this awareness through diligent work, and thus becomes fully human. Mystics work, practice, devote, and dedicate themselves to the great challenge of first seeing and then being who they are, essentially, beneath the veils of thinking and limited identities. A mystic's path wends through the limitations of conditioning, superstition and belief, the dark nests of troubling desires, fears, dependencies and attachments, false idols and mistaken identities. A mystic's path cuts right through delusion and ignorance toward reality's panoramic grandeur.

A mystic is not some special person endowed with superhuman virtue or sanctity, but a person who consciously seeks significance in living. In seeking significance, *meaning,* they put their own personal borders and barricades at risk in the mystery and invite awe, wonder, exhilaration, depth, silence, beauty, and love to overrun them. They are willing to be taken by the breath within the breath. They sleep on the exposed cliff face, looking down at Yosemite Valley, high and vulnerable to the light of sudden beauty and revelation.

A person in love is spiritual. A person who disappears while watching a hawk's wings dip and slice the invisible currents is spiritual. A person holding an infant for the first time is spiritual. A person worshiping at the feet of redwoods or wading in glacial lakes is spiritual. In all these instances, and countless others, we notice there is a moment in which we leave ourselves and enter something larger. We become the beauty we behold; we lose ourselves as one, and then find ourselves in all. This is not an uncommon experience. This is the portal of reality: leaving the contours of the small self for the grand wilderness of love, of beauty, of unity.

Mystics are not a special class of people, possessing powers and insights unavailable to the rest of us. We are all mystics. Mysticism is simply the recognition of what is truly significant about living.

Mysticism is the art of the real, and mystics are people who seek to know the real. As we become acquainted with, then know, then intimately love reality, an automatic reordering of our values occurs. Reality itself imparts this order, and this order unveils a banquet of sweet significance. Our every impulse is a product manufactured by reality itself. Our lives and our legacies are thus made beautiful as we become the helpmates of reality.

However, mysticism has gotten a bum rap from a popular culture which seems to have become entranced by the unreal. Even dictionaries are equivocal: they define mysticism as "direct, immediate, intimate communion with ultimate reality." Then those same dictionaries describe mysticism as "vague and groundless speculation" or something "cryptic, unintelligible, and obscure." The resolution of this paradox is crucial, for if we—as individuals, communities, and societies—are to relieve the tensions, burdens, and complex problems snarling at our heels, we had better understand the nature of reality. "What is real?" is the single most important question we can ask. We should not be afraid that this inquiry into reality will lead us astray, or that our search will be irrelevant.

The resolution of this paradox can be found in the same dictionaries that present the paradox. Mysticism, reality, is unintelligible to the faculties of reason and intellect. However, reality is eminently perceptible and knowable, if we first travel deep into the uncontrollable wilderness of heart and soul, of wonder and awe, of silence and being. To know reality, we must abandon our addiction to rational analysis in favor of intuitive insight. We have to see ourselves and our world with an innocence uncorrupted by the false certainties of our ideas and beliefs. We must touch the actual heat of reality with the same immediacy of feeling as when placing our palm, open and facedown, on a glowing stovetop.

I don't know anyone who is not interested in the significance of what is ultimately real, meaningful, and beautiful. Mysticism is the well from which we can draw the water of true values. It is that space where we learn of significance and meaning, where we learn to live in accord with and in service to universal truths, truths which have been affirmed and ratified by mystics from every society and culture which has ever existed.

I am saddened at mysticism's bum rap, because it has caused us to become suspicious of what is real and meaningful. We have created a society with de facto values and principles which are starkly antithetical to mystical feelings.

The spiritual message of the mystics is simple, clear, and universal. Their voices are our voices. They have an important message for leaders everywhere, for those who want to lead from a knowledge of what is seen and known on the mountaintops of timelessness. The mystics' message is this: it is important to know who we are, essentially, by directly perceiving our true nature. All things in this world are alive and conscious, deserving of our respect and care. Love and wisdom arise naturally in the experience of our oneness with life.

We are all mystics to the degree that the experience of "oneness"—not as an idea but as a living fact—is awake and active within us.

Wouldn't you like to legitimize conversations about mystical reality—about significance, love, silence, beauty, and consciousness—in offices and meeting rooms throughout America and the world?

For Personal Reflection

Place a clean pad of paper and a pen in front of you. At the top of the page, write: "Spiritual People I Know." Take a few minutes to quiet your mind and relax your body. Reflect on the people you have known. Think about someone whom you believe to be a spiritual person. Begin writing about this person. Do not edit your thoughts. Do not judge your thoughts. Simply write. When you are finished, read what you have written. What does this person tell you? What does this person teach you about the qualities and characteristics of spiritual living?

Ask yourself if these same qualities are within you. Think of times when you feel that you are a spiritual person. Write about such times. Do not compare yourself to anyone else; just write about your own experience of being spiritual. Let your writing show you the ways in which you are a spiritual person. Simply learn about yourself.

6

Mystical Experience

Twenty-five years ago, I was living in an ashram, a meditation center, in India. One morning, around 5:30, I walked out of the kitchen in which I had been cleaning and cutting fruits and vegetables for the communal lunch. The sun was just rising above the mountain ridge across the valley. I sat on a concrete planter that surrounded several coconut trees and fell into meditation.

My head became heavy with silence, my thoughts subsided, and my body began to dissolve. I remained aware, but that awareness was not located within me. Awareness penetrated me from all directions. Everything was alive, everything was breathing with awareness. A moment later, I entered the breath of all things and disappeared.

In that breath was a white light. It emanated from everything. It was everywhere. In the leaves and flowers, the stone walls, the clumps of dirt, the muddy water, the people passing by. There was an awareness of breathing and light, yet no perceiver, no body, no self—and tremendous order and intelligence! There was such precision and purpose—each thing related exquisitely to the next—everything defined within itself and in relation to everything else, ordered and sustained by the breathing and the light which had no source but was everywhere, streaming, busy, and yet unmoving.

That experience lasted for two days, after which I did not want to talk for a long time.

The residue of that experience is with me to this day. I know that I embrace all of life within me, and I am, in turn, embraced by all of life. Sometimes I cry when the utter peace of this light returns. I know the world is a condensation of this breath, and that we are all particles of this light.

It is this light which gives beauty and significance to all things. It is this light which binds everything together. This light is the breath of love. This light is the consciousness that pervades the entire universe. This is who we are.

That was one of many experiences I've had over the years that carried me across the threshold of the spiritual world. The word "spirit" is a loaded word in our culture, as is the word "soul". There are many places in which we do not use these words, or use them advisedly. One reason is that we do not want to offend those whose definitions of spirit and soul are different from ours. Another reason is fear: we are afraid that powers greater than us will judge us as flakes, incompetents, or cultists. For the sake of these and other reasons, we often hide the spiritual side of our lives in ghettos.

Huston Smith, the eminent professor, author, and sage, brings needed clarity to the nature of this experience of self-transcendence. He says there are four universal characteristics embedded in the mystical nexus of all spiritual paths and philosophies.

The first is ineffability, which means that the experience is difficult to accurately portray in words. The best we can do is to use poetry, image, metaphor, or music. We cannot describe it directly because words do not travel that far.

The second is unity, which means we feel connected to, or part of, something larger than our own body/mind. It's as though our boundaries of self slip and slide away until they embrace the whole of creation.

The third is immense joy. The sudden encounter with grace lifts us to dizzying heights of bliss and ecstasy. The thrill of peace opens our inner eye to mysteries previously unseen.

The fourth characteristic is certitude. One is convinced that what one beholds is true—the way things are. This certitude is beyond reproach, beyond proof, beyond sentiment. We find ourselves standing in the oceanic rhythms of reality.

To these four characteristics, I would add a fifth: wholeness. Surrounded and permeated by spirit, we experience ourselves as complete, full, and without lack of any kind. Nothing in the form of experience, knowledge, or material goods can enhance the wholeness we feel. In that moment, nothing is missing.

We have the seeds of this kind of transcendent humanity within us. We have all known such moments of surpassing beauty and unity, and we know this is real. We have only decided to live in lesser ways.

Emanuel Swedenborg said, "The divine Essence itself is love and wisdom." What more do we need than to realize that we are that divine Essence? Wisdom and love are the twin formless faces of the soul.

This treasure of self-transcendence is what God wants for us. It is the answer to our prayers for sanity, harmony, balance, peace, and prosperity. This answer is the love which saturates every atom of the universe, if only we would see, feel, touch, hear, and smell this distilled essence of life.

The treasure of self-transcendence is the context in which all of our other activities and pursuits must be placed. The bottom line of life must be drawn with the pen and ink of the Creator, who wishes for us to consecrate our every action toward the realization of soul.

The simple fact is that we cannot live without the soul. We have to free our souls from servitude to lesser gods, from lesser purposes, and feast together at the banquet set and ready for us.

In an interview with James Lipton on the *Bravo* television show, *Inside the Actor's Studio,* Sharon Stone told of sitting with her acting teacher, Roy London, during his final days. Dying of AIDS, he would lapse in and out of consciousness. One time, he opened his eyes and said, "It's so beautiful. It's so beautiful. It's all about love. I only wish I could teach one more class."

Must we wait until we are taking our last breaths to remember to live what we already know: that life is about love, not fear; selflessness, not self-interest?

Transcendence does not remove us from daily life; rather, it connects us to all of life. Transcendence does not leave us incapable, but more capable. Transcendence does not destroy intelligence, but imbues intelligence with wisdom.

Mahatma Gandhi said, "I do not believe that the spiritual law works on a field of its own. On the contrary, it expresses itself only through the ordinary activities of life. It thus affects the economic, the social and the political fields."

Václav Havel, the president of the Czech Republic, says emphatically, "Yes, the only real hope of people today is probably a renewal of our certainty that we are rooted in the Earth and, at the same time, in the cosmos. This awareness endows us with the capacity for self-transcendence. Politicians at international forums may reiterate a thousand times that the basis of the new world order must be universal respect for human rights, but it will mean nothing as long as this imperative does not derive from the respect of the miracle of Being, the miracle of the universe, the miracle of nature, the miracle of our own existence. Only someone who submits to the authority of the universal order and of creation, who values the right to be a part of it and a participant in it, can genuinely value himself and his neighbors, and thus honor their rights as well."

Submitting to the universal order is a simple matter of admitting that we live within a soulful universe.

For Personal Reflection

Place a pen and a clean pad of paper in front of you. At the top of the page, write: "A Spiritual Experience I Have Had." Take a few minutes to quiet your mind and relax your body. Reflect on your life. Let your inner mind take you to a time and place in which you experienced your own soul. Begin writing about it. Do not edit your thoughts. Do not judge your thoughts. Simply write.

When you are finished, read what you have written. What does this experience tell you? What does this experience teach you about meaning and purpose? Ask yourself if you are living consistently with what you know to be true.

Ask yourself if you ever betray this knowledge. If you answer yes, take up your pen and begin to write down all the reasons you do. Do not judge yourself. Simply learn.

7
Inner Guidance

Almost 15 years ago, I went on a week-long vision quest in Mexico. I slept in a small hotel in a fishing village whose name I've forgotten. During the day, I would walk the beach, sitting down from time to time to stare at the horizon with one set of eyes and, with another set, to follow my breath to its lair. In the evening, I would drink beer and eat grilled shrimp, reflecting on the day's meditations.

I went on this trip to meditate and reflect on my work. Something was out of kilter with either the *what* or the *how* of my work life. I was leaking life force, which is to say that I was becoming spiritually depressed. I needed guidance.

At that time, I was a consultant whose clients were mainly senior executives in small to mid-sized corporations. My role as a "clarity coach" was to enhance my clients' awareness of themselves and their relationships. As a function of my own years of training in mindfulness, I could usually see and point out some crucial aspect of a relationship or situation that no one else could see, and those insights would then empower my clients to realize their goals and purposes. I enjoyed my work and my clients were pleased with my contributions. Still, I felt a malaise and sadness within my true heart.

My true heart had developed during the decade previous to my consulting career, while I studied spiritual science with a meditation master. During most of those years, including four spent in India, I was shaken by personal earthquakes of inner awakening. I had discovered exotic and profound worlds within myself and, as a consequence, experienced a steady reshaping of the view of reality that had been bequeathed to me by various authorities as I was growing up. The essence of my true heart was in the continuous exploration of inner consciousness and its expression in the world.

I suspected that in supporting my clients' efforts, I was somehow neglecting the core of my true heart, which had been aroused and forged in those earthquakes of my formative years. I may have taken on too much of my clients' reality in order to be of service to them. My clients were primarily interested in business success; I was primarily interested in the silent depths of inner revelation. I felt that I wasn't breathing the air I was meant to breathe and was slowly suffocating. The vivid light of creation was dimming. So I did what I always do when I feel blocked, conflicted, or out of alignment: I went inward.

Going inward through meditation and self-inquiry is a superior adventure: one never knows what one will find or the degree to which what is found will impact or transform one's life. Perhaps some will wonder whether this "going inward" is an appropriate solution to life's conflicts and dilemmas. For me it is, in all cases, the first and most important thing to do. The silence I find at my center is the voice of my soul, and it is that voice I listen to and follow. I usually augment what I hear in silence, later, with my intellect—analyzing, planning, coordinating, and so on—but I must receive the first impulse, the primal vision, from the indwelling silence.

On the fourth day of my quest, the voice of silence spoke wordlessly and unequivocally: *Teach the mysticism you know to leaders.* My initial reaction was terror. No way! I didn't want to do that. That was 15 years ago, when words like "spirit" and "soul" had barely found their way into the business lexicon. I also felt that, in spite of almost 20 years of spiritual practice and study, I knew less than when I began and was losing more ground every day. I felt it would be a nut too hard to crack, causing me to die of ridicule and starvation, and I said so.

Do it, said the voice, *and you will be guided. It is your path.*

I remember drinking a dozen or so beers that night. The following day, I went back to the beach. I sat silently and waited for a confirming conversation, which was not long in coming. *Teach the essence of hamsa to world leaders. Don't worry.* I protested. *Hamsa?* Why not just put a gun to my head and pull the trigger? *Hamsa* is a Sanskrit word which means "supreme transcendent wisdom." *Hamsa* is a mantra that signifies our unity with that consciousness which pervades every atom of this universe and connects all living beings. I was supposed to talk to leaders about *that?* It's one thing to talk about mysticism, consciousness, and meditation with like-minded people; hell, I had lived in one spiritual ghetto or another for almost 20 years. I could certainly talk that talk. But in corporate boardrooms? With senators and presidents, with moguls and magnates?

I drank many beers that night and chased each one with a tequila shot—or was it the other way around—trying to come to grips with this "vision." I knew that resistance was out of the question—what's the point of spending a lifetime loosening the vocal chords of that small, still voice if one is not going to listen and follow? Still, I was terrified. I knew intuitively that it was a path that would require me to encounter my every fear, insecurity, doubt, pretense, and delusion.

It was one thing to be a consultant who drew privately on spiritual practice and principles to help roll clients' wheels along the path of their aspirations; it was another thing altogether to stand for and speak about "unity with the cosmos." I began to hyperventilate, afraid of things unseen and unknown. My spiritual teacher said, "To understand *hamsa* is to experience our unity with the cosmos." Talk about an intimidating mission statement!

Upon returning home to Mill Valley, California, I began to convert the townhouse I was renting into a retreat center and to tell friends and associates what I was up to. The ones who didn't laugh looked at me carefully for a long time, trying to decide if it was really me, or someone else. It didn't take a psychic to know what they were thinking: "Hmmm, it must have been some bad fish, or maybe the water. He'll be okay in a few days."

Even those colleagues who shared my spiritual inclinations advised me against being so bold. Better to say something that will get you in the front door, and then slowly reveal your real work, they said. Better to advertise high performance team building, visionary leadership, or something they can get their hands on and their minds around.

I remember having dinner with my best friend and his wife, both of whom almost yelled, "Are you fucking nuts? Nobody in business wants that." Remember, that was 15 years ago. I didn't disagree with them. But I couldn't betray myself, either. I knew that avoidance would be far more painful than experiencing whatever fears and trepidations I had. I would just have to go in the direction that silence had pointed out. A dear friend of mine once said that if we never leap from the precipice of our fears and attachments, we'll never find out whether the soul-force of the universe might catch us.

Shortly after my return from Mexico, I had the first opportunity to publicly test my vision. I had agreed, before going to Mexico, to deliver a morning talk to the legal affairs department of a billion-dollar pharmaceutical company. As I was unpacking my briefcase, the people began to file in: one three-piece gray suit after another. One or two wore break-set white vertical stripes, looking vaguely like gangsters from a 1930s movie.

The head of the department came over and asked for my card. Returning to his seat, he looked at my card, which now had the word *hamsa* on it, and asked, "What the hell does *hamsa* mean?"

This is it, I thought. They're going to throw me out on my ass. I actually began putting my notes, pens, and markers back into my briefcase.

"*Hamsa*," I said, "means supreme, transcendent wisdom."

The attorney's face tensed and his head fell forward into his hands. As he shook his head back and forth, I closed my briefcase and prepared to leave. But then he looked up.

"My God," he sighed, "do we ever need some of that around here."

For Personal Reflection

Place a pen and a clean pad of paper in front of you. At the top of the page, write: "Inner Guidance I Have Received." Take a few minutes to quiet your mind and relax your body. Reflect on your life. Let your inner mind take you to a time in which you were confused about which way to turn or what to do next. See if you remember hearing some voice or urge from within directing you. Begin writing about it. Do not edit your thoughts. Do not judge your thoughts. Simply write.

When you are finished, read what you have written. What does this experience tell you? Did you follow this inner guidance? If you did, what happened? If you didn't, why not? Write about both. Do not judge yourself. Simply learn.

8

The Real World

Over the years, I've had many close encounters of a mystical kind. Some were very powerful and took me years to integrate. Some were pleasant, some beatific, and some were terrifying.

I've been transported out of time. I've stepped out of my body as from a pile of dirty clothes and drifted in light. Once, in meditation, I went to the center of the Earth and heard Her breathe. I've been stopped dead in my tracks by an overwhelming feeling of love, my eyes misting over, heart crumbling, wanting to touch every single person, every living creature, with gratitude and tenderness. I've seen the light that is the life of all things, which comes from someplace—from where, I don't know. I have glided as in a sailplane over landscapes from other worlds. I've sat on God's front porch while meditating in my own backyard and felt the tremors of new creation. I've been demolished by a silence and peace, by an expansiveness, for which I haven't a single word of description. These experiences expanded my awareness of the many dimensions and facets of reality, and profoundly affected my perception of reality.

I used to lead a weekly class in Mill Valley. People would come by, we'd meditate for a while, and then I'd usually give a talk, followed by some lively dialogue with whoever showed up. There was a core group of people who came nearly every week, including one young woman who drove up from San Jose, a three-hour round-trip. She would follow along for a while, sinking into her own silence and breathing, happy to let go of herself and her ideas. But then something in her would snap and she would bark, "What does this have to do with reality?"

She understood me—up to a point, and I understood her—up to a point. What we were speaking about then—and what we're speaking about now—is that mystery of incomparable depths and dimensions called reality. My friend's reality was limited to what she could see, feel, control, and affect. She was always most interested in finding new strategies to get her way, to realize her ambitions, to get and to have. She talked of mastering her life; I talked of serving life. That young woman was a perfect example of a person who was reality challenged. Our society has built a single-lane road of materialism for us to use as we travel through reality. No wonder there's so much traffic and so many accidents!

The world that is perceptible to our senses and the world of our concepts and beliefs are certainly parts of reality, but they're so tiny as to barely be blips on the screen. Unless what conventional society calls the real world is put into the proper context and perspective, it is no more than a dream. A dream. A mystic knows this. Spiritual experiences help to loosen our grip on the dominant materialistic view of reality. They help us to expand the boundaries of who we think we are.

We must each find our connection with reality through our own investigation of self, mind, and reality. The mystical experience is a wild sea in which wave upon wave of depth and significance crash over us; layers, facets, and dimensions of the great mystery open and befriend us. It is, as John Lee Hooker said, "Yes! Yes! So sweet!"

The mysticism I know is simple: it is the silence that falls upon us in a moment of beauty, creation, love, communion, or deep reflection.

The word "mysticism" has come, colloquially, to represent the arcane, the abstract, the remote, and mysterious. However, the exact opposite is true. It means, literally, to experience an immediate connection with life itself. But as simple as that sounds, a lot can get in the way of our experience of life. We have to be reminded, awakened, or jolted into a recollection of the obvious and self-evident simplicity that mysticism implies.

Within each person is a depth of being that is silent, and that silence embraces the entire universe: rock, salamander, iris, and sun. The experience of silence is exquisite and so different from our conventional mode of experience that it can scarcely be spoken about, let alone taught as most things are taught. There are many paths to silence. My path took me to the East, to India, where I studied with a meditation master. I learned that silence is the great teacher, the great explainer, the great illuminator. Silence is chronic, compulsive intuition and spontaneity. It is a light spring rain from a cloudless sky, beyond the reach of the mind. That rain is spiritual nourishment to all living things—and all things are living.

Mysticism refers to the self-transcendent clarity that is found in silence, love, beauty, the explosive aftermath of poetry and music, the awesome fact of forests and mountains, the revelry of lovemaking and carnivals of eroticism, the rhythms of dance, and the cadence of song, chant, and prayer. The mystic is in love with that which will not brook any formulation. Mysticism cannot be turned into principles and paradigms. It is too free, endlessly creative, and joyful for any of that.

The mystic language is not meant to inform, convince, or persuade; the words are like missiles, meant to stop the mind with a judder, to collapse reason, time, and self. In the collapsed rubble, spontaneity lurks, and the silence-infested clarity of reality purrs loudly.

The best I can do, by way of teaching what can't be taught, is to invoke silence. This silence is of utmost importance, much more so than anything I or anyone else can say. The mysticism I know, I can only point to: an exquisite silence which can be directly experienced within the deep core of each human being. This inner silence is itself the true seat of power and teacher of wisdom. I learn from this silence. I see from this silence. Silence opens the heart and clears the mind. I trust this silence to provide clarity, courage, and truth. This is what I trust, and this is what I know inheres in each person: a clear mind and an open heart. It is not enough to agree or disagree; in order to be authentic, the indwelling silent beauty must be realized by each one of us. Otherwise, we will be merely the stooges of gossip, rumor, and reality by agreement.

The French film director Jean-Jacques Annaud, in describing his work, said, "I want my images to carry an emotion you can hardly describe with words. They ring a secret bell in your heart, and those are the bells I love to ring."

The secret bell I love to ring is silence. It is my hope that something in this book will arouse your own inner silence, and that this aroused silence will cause you to contemplate who you are, at your essence, and to reflect upon what you are doing, how you are doing it, and why. The essence of mysticism is really the essence of significance: it is a values-based approach to life in which one's values are inspired by a direct and immediate experience of transcendent reality. To be a mystic is to belong to life itself and to live amid its continuous eruption of silence and beauty. It is to be joined with life beneath the shells and surfaces of the visible, to swim in the invisible depths, to travel deep into the subterranean caverns of suspended breath, to climb the exalted high peaks of snow-blind rapture, and finally, to return to the porches of our homes where we sit contentedly with the ones we love, and in so loving, loving all. How is this obscure? How is this irrelevant?

For Personal Reflection

Take a few minutes to reflect on your life. Have you experienced an episode of self-transcendence, a moment in which your habitual self dissolved into a greater experience of being? It may have been while walking through the woods, playing with your children, or listening to music. Spend some time writing about that experience, letting the many facets of it come out in words.

What does that experience tell you about significance and meaning? What does that experience tell you about your life, its nature and purpose? To what extent has that experience fully entered your life? Have you spoken about such experiences with others?

9
Dear Mr. Balsekar

About a dozen years ago, I heard that Ramesh S. Balsekar was coming to Mill Valley, California, where I lived, and would be holding a few *satsangs*—meetings for the purpose of inquiring into truth—with students and other interested people. This was great news, as Balsekar had been the translator of Nisargadatta Maharaj, a well-known mystic who lived in Bombay and who had influenced many seekers with his unforgiving style of inquiry. In addition, Balsekar had been an executive with the Bank of India. I thought he would be a perfect person with whom to speak about mysticism and its application to the business world.

I attended one of his *satsangs,* which was held in a private home in Tiburon. The next day, I went back to the same house to meet with Balsekar privately. He was very polite and gracious as he escorted me to a small patio. We sat on chairs, separated by a round table with a glass top.

In the course of our conversation, I spoke about a book idea that was in my mind at that time, about meditation and self-inquiry for business leaders. He listened intently, and then asked, "So you want to write a book about meditation, self-inquiry, and self-knowledge for the businessman. Is that correct?"

"Yes, that is correct."

"Why?" His tone was direct and matter-of-fact.

I confess that I had not asked myself that question. I just assumed everyone, businesspeople included, wanted to know the truth about themselves and the world. I asked Balsekar how his own interest in self-inquiry and pursuit of inner knowing had influenced his career as an executive with the Bank of India.

"Not at all," he said. He explained that it was only after his retirement that he began to get serious about self-inquiry.

He continued with a series of questions. "Why should businesspeople read this book? How will it help them in their business? A businessman is not interested in truth. A businessman is interested in profit. Is your book going to help him make a profit?"

His questions were good business questions: Who is your market? What need does your product fill? How will you position and sell it? Balsekar seemed to be reminding me that the first and main questions of a businessperson are related to how to make money.

After our conversation, I reflected. Of course, business leaders *would* wonder at the practicality of spiritual inquiry and discovery. Would a deeper and clearer understanding of the human spirit, the nature of mind, and the power of consciousness really have contact points with the day-to-day demands of running a business? Is the subtle realm of spiritual insight really useful and relevant in a business context?

I took Balsekar's questions to heart. I love questions and respect them, particularly those which disturb one's status quo. The first word I ever spoke was *why*. That predisposition toward inquiry has remained with me to this day.

The kinds of questions one asks are very powerful, very defining. They will take us in one direction or another. They will create our path in life. The questions I asked earlier in life, such as "Who am I?" and "What is real?" pulled me out into deep waters. They were siren songs, leading to great adventures and near disasters. My questions propelled me to run with the bulls in Pamplona, to roam in Finnish Lapland, to prowl the cafes of Paris and jazz clubs of Frankfurt, to wander in the deserts of Israel, to seek visions in the hashish dens of Afghanistan, and finally to learn about meditation and the wonders of the inner life in an ashram in India.

"Who am I?" This is one kind of question. It's the kind of question that leads inward to silence, dissolution, and experiences that cannot be truly described.

"How will I make money?" This is another kind of question. This kind of question leads to other questions of the same genus: Do I have a business and marketing plan? Do I have sufficient capitalization? Do I have a capable management team? This line of questioning leads to answers, decisions, commitment, actions, and results.

My reply to Balsekar was that a businessperson should be interested in truth because first things come first.

First things come first. Are we businesspeople, or are we first human beings? Are we a Democrat or Republican, or are we first a human being? Are we Chinese or Tibetan, or are we first a human being? Are we white, black, or red, or are we first a human being? Are we male or female, or are we first a human being? Are we Jews, Catholics, Hindus, or Moslems, or are we first a human being? Are we fat, thin, rich, or poor, or are we first a human being?

First things first. We are first human beings. Human *being* is the context from which we must evaluate all the roles we play in life.

A few years ago, I accompanied an executive team to the Green Gulch Zen Center in Mill Valley, California, for a three-day retreat. Our agenda was to review corporate goals, renew commitments, and strengthen relationships. Well after the first day's session had concluded, somewhere around 1:30 A.M., one of the division vice presidents and I began speaking about his recent vacation.

The others had gone to sleep. He and I were sitting on a futon, his face barely visible in the light of the fire's last embers. He told me how one morning he had roused his wife and three sons and how they had gone together, before the sun was up, to sit on the rim of the Grand Canyon. They sat together, holding hands in silence, their feet dangling in the abyss, watching the sun come up. He tried to say more about that moment but he couldn't.

Instead, his breathing elongated and his eyes narrowed, as though he were seeing into an indescribable distance. I could feel the presence within him and surrounding him. He spread giant wings and yet remained seated and still.

After many silent moments, he said, simply, "I love my family more than anything. I want to live in that love."

Have you ever sat with your feet dangling in the cosmic abyss and been consumed by a presence, a force, an encompassing state of being? Here, in the early morning, as the sun comes upon the water-crafted canyons, we are able to see without stop, across boundaries into the distance that cannot be spoken. Something is revealed here, some form of wordless knowing that transcends ambiguity and relativity. The word my client used to represent this experience was love. We all want to live in the love, because it is in this living that we find our wholeness and our totality. In this revelation of our unity with all things, we find a clarity of conscience which becomes the context for our human being.

A businessperson, I told Balsekar, should be interested in meditation, self-inquiry, and self-knowledge because these pursuits unfold the truest expression of our human *being:* love. We must remember the once known, the twice known, but frequently forgotten essential context of human being: *I want to live in that love.*

Within this context, the first question will not be about how to make money. If this is the first question, something is wrong. Our business activities must exist within the context of our heart's great longing to know its own deep source. Without this as our context, we can only misquote the nature of reality and pervert the truth of who we are, thus wandering through life as soulless ghosts whose only appetite is for money.

So we must ask the question, "What is a human being?" To answer this question will give depth and dimension, value and significance, meaning and purpose to being in business.

As we open ourselves and embrace the power and presence of love, we forge a new alliance with life and work. Instead of meeting in conference rooms and airless cubicles, we will meet together every day on the rims of ancient canyons, celebrating that which comes first, before all else.

For Personal Reflection

Do you feel that the primary purpose of business is to make money, or do you feel that business should exist as a means to serve something else? Can we live a truthful life at work if our business activity is disconnected from our inner spiritual life and understanding?

10

The Source of Skill

The main tool in my consultant's toolbox is clarity, the ability to see behind what appears to be happening in order to discern what is actually happening. I can't think of a single situation where this tool was not the first, and usually the only, tool I have used. Clarity is part attention, part listening, part openness, and part patience. The biggest part of clarity, though, is inner silence, which occurs in the total release of thoughts, images, beliefs, and reactions. From this inner silence, the most appropriate course of action is revealed.

Many years ago, I had the pleasure of meeting Judith Skutch-Whitson, publisher of *A Course of Miracles*. She told me the following story:

> A long time ago, I was teaching parapsychology at New York University, and in one of my classes was a young man attached to the Venezuelan Embassy. We became good friends and one day my young friend told me that he and the Venezuelan ambassador had sometimes discussed parapsychology and spirit. He also said that the ambassador wanted to meet me.
>
> At that time, the ambassador was considered to be a mediator par excellence; anytime there was a problem anywhere in the United Nations, he was called upon to mediate the dispute.

One day we met for lunch. He was a silver-haired, dapper gentleman who kissed my hand and made me feel instantly like a queen. We had a grand lunch, talking about parapsychology and psychic research. He told me he was very hungry to talk about these things, but could not seem to find people in his own environment who had similar ideas. I told him I knew two people who held a mystic circle in the UN. We each had the feeling that one of the purposes of our meeting was for me to introduce him to like-minded people.

I asked him how he originally got involved in this kind of thinking. He said, "Many years ago, I was sent to France for my education. One of my teachers was an old Jewish philosopher, a very gifted man, who gave me a very precious gift. He taught me how to quiet myself, a method of inner meditation, a process by which I could touch the deep inner core of my being."

I was, of course, very interested and asked him if he could give me an example of how or when he would do this. He replied, "I had a two-week assignment in Paris. It was a very gloomy winter week and I had to get the leaders of forty-three Third World countries to agree on twenty-four principles of action for the United Nations. There were so many different languages, even many dialects within the languages of the contingents from certain countries, and for the first week the meeting was an absolute cacophony of disaster.

"No one was speaking to anyone else. It was dreary and cold. The room wasn't well ventilated, people were smoking, coughing, and wheezing, and no one was listening to anyone else. I felt as if I were a total failure and wondered what to do.

"All of a sudden, the face of that Jewish philosopher appeared before me and I remembered that I had forgotten the precious gift he had given me so many years ago. I had forgotten to do the technique he had taught me. I closed my eyes for a few moments. I took a few deep breaths and I went deep, deep, deep into my interior, where I really live. I asked for help about what to do. A voice said to me, Open your eyes and let your eyes go around the room, seeing each person and surrounding them with light. I slowly opened my eyes and began to do as I had been instructed.

"I looked at each of the delegates, slowly and one at a time, surrounding them with light and broadcasting the thought: I love you.

"It took about half an hour. I was so intent upon my process that I

didn't notice when the level of noise receded. It was very interesting. The delegates began actually talking and listening in a manner that I had not seen during the entire first week. I wondered what I should do next, so I again closed my eyes and took a few deep breaths, asking in the deep interior of my being for guidance. The voice said, Ask them all to stop and be silent.

"I opened my eyes and said, 'Ladies and gentlemen, I've been sitting here quietly watching all this go on, and I realize that we are not getting anywhere. We have twenty-four issues to decide upon and we haven't yet agreed upon even one. I know each of you has a culture which recognizes creation as being far greater than the individual person, and I know that in your own homes you celebrate that idea. I would like to offer the opportunity of a five-minute silence, during which I would like to ask everyone to touch that part of him- or herself wherein that spirit lives and ask how we might best proceed.'

"No one disagreed. I asked that the lights be dimmed, and we all closed our eyes for five minutes. And then a miracle happened. When we opened our eyes, that room was filled with light. Everyone saw it and gasped. No lights had gone on, the sun hadn't come out, but that room was full of light.

"Within two hours we had come up with a plan on how to approach the twenty-four issues. We went home two days early, having accomplished our mission."

Here is a man who was much honored for his ability and achievements, and they never knew why. He never told anyone that the source of his skill came from an old Jewish philosopher who had explained to him where our oneness lies and how to touch that sacred place.

You and I are not different from this silence and light, and when we know who we are, we will know what to do.

For Personal Reflection

Have you ever used a similar approach in your work? What were the results? If not, would you be willing to initiate such a process? What fears come up as you contemplate this possibility? Can you see the potential benefits for initiating such a process in your workplace?

11

The New Species

We start playing follow the leader as kids, and we never stop. Now, as grownups, the game has higher stakes. Before we give our allegiance to a leader, we need to clearly understand what we want our leaders to do, and to be. We can't just blindly follow Susie or Timmy or Johnny or Elizabeth because they happen to be at the front of the line. If we take the time to really investigate the mystique of leadership, we may find that we ourselves are the leaders we want to follow.

Leadership is like a *koan,* one of those insoluble Zen riddles that are used to confound the mind and drive one into a spontaneous realization of truth. When you take your hard-won answer to Zen masters, they are likely to bust you over the head in disgust. NOT EVEN CLOSE! Back to the mat you go. Day after day, you bring your answer to the riddle for the Zen master's approval. Day after day, you are rebuked and sent away. No answer or definition will ever be approved. Only a spontaneous outpouring of intuition and freedom will be approved. But we're not Zen students here, so let's attempt some definition of leadership. Maybe we can sneak one by the Zen master.

There are scores of leadership definitions, each with its own set of characteristics, qualities, and goals. Concepts of leadership are constantly evolving as our culture evolves. Any concept of leadership is heavily dependent upon context; leaders are defined and evaluated in terms of their purposes and goals: a military commander wins medals for leadership that would be unthinkable on a mindfulness walk through a meadow. There are over 40 synonyms for leadership in my dictionary, and each one differs significantly in nuances of meaning and context. We could stock a bookstore with books on leadership. We can spend a fortune attending leadership seminars and conferences, listening to audiotapes, and watching video programs that present leading edge techniques, models, theories, and paradigms to develop our leadership potential.

We can try to define leadership with adjectives. Stop by the business section of your neighborhood bookstore, and you will find leadership styles of various colors and textures: *visionary, passionate, spiritual, authentic, charismatic, practical.* The pantheon of leadership gurus whose works we can study includes Jesus Christ and Warren Bennis, Machiavelli and Stephen Covey, Genghis Khan and Margaret Wheatley, Sun Tzu and Robert K. Greenleaf.

We can try to distinguish leadership from management. We can say that management is about organizing, planning, implementing, and controlling; and leadership is about vision, values, and spirit. Using this distinction, we can go on and try to refine the characteristics, attitudes, and behaviors of a leader. A few years ago, an article in the *San Francisco Chronicle* described the results of a survey of 250 senior executives, showing that the leadership characteristic held in highest regard was the ability to get results. Those results were understandable, of course, because we so often turn to leaders to solve our problems.

Even this cursory inquiry into leadership reveals that the leadership elephant is too big for anyone to get their arms completely around. Anything we say about leadership can only be a description of the part of that elephant we are touching, and not the whole elephant.

In our society, a leader is most often defined as a person having the kind of authority that either commands or influences other people. The source of that authority might be political or organizational, such as that of a president, governor, or CEO. It might be religious, as in the case of a priest or rabbi. A leader's authority and influence might come from their wealth, celebrity, or social pedigree.

In addition to the obvious leaders, like President Bush and Colin Powell, we could say that Bob Dylan and Barbra Streisand are leaders. Bill Gates and Anita Roddick are leaders, as are Susan Sarandon and Martin Scorsese and Jody Foster. Ozzy Osborne and Bonnie Raitt are leaders. Larry Flynt, Jerry Falwell, and Louis Farrakhan are leaders, as are Michael Jordan, Lisa Leslie, and Martina Navratilova. Donna Karan and Giorgio Armani are leaders, as are Oprah Winfrey and Maya Angelou. Deepak Chopra, Bernie Siegel, and Marianne Williamson are leaders. Barbara Walters, Larry King, Howard Stern, and Norman Lear are leaders, as is Stephen Hawking.

These leaders—defined by their ability to influence others—live in every sector of our society: government, entertainment, business, media, sports, religion, science, education, medicine, health, and the military. These leaders have high visibility, either locally or nationally, and their statements are heard and considered.

The influence that these people have helps to define the reality of those whom they influence. They might define our philosophy and values, our lifestyle, our aesthetic; they might define our product choices, or for whom we vote. They might ask us to open our eyes to new possibilities, or to keep our eyes closed. These leaders, by their words and actions, affect our attitudes about everything: politics and foreign policy, money, art, sex, death, race and gender issues, relationships and marriage, ethics and morality, work, diet and health, spirituality, religion, heaven and hell, animal rights, and on and on. In all cases, a leader's influence in some measure defines our reality, whether or not we embrace a particular point of view; rejecting someone's point of view can just as easily help shape and define our values and priorities.

These leaders may be wise and intelligent or they may be ignorant and stupid. They may serve the common welfare, or they may bilk unsuspecting people out of billions of dollars. They may tell the truth, or they may be habitual liars. They may be chaste swans and mate for life, or they may be intrepid sexual adventurers. Having influence is no guarantee of anything; it just means some people will listen and, in many cases, follow.

I think we *should* expect some guarantees about who and what a leader is. Leaders should be committed to the common good, not just special interests. Leaders should tell the truth, and not spin preposterous lies that obscure their motives and actions. Leaders should consider the short- and long-term consequences of their actions, and by long-term, I mean 500 years. Leaders should respect life and should serve and protect all living things. Leaders should be creative, able to come up with ideas and solutions that have never been seen or tried before. Where is the great leadership vision and intelligence behind going to war? Haven't we seen the futility of this too many times? Leaders should be curious and continuously learning; they should associate with all kinds of people from many cultures so they can become rich and exotic through diverse influences. Leaders should be comfortable with their bodies; they should be able to enjoy pleasure, and not be the indentured slaves of fear, shame, and guilt. Leaders should explore the spiritual realm of life.

But there is something over and above all of this that we should expect from our leaders.

We should expect them to know reality.

Nisargadatta Maharaj, an Indian mystic, said, "When more people come to know their real nature, their influence, however subtle, will prevail and the world's emotional atmosphere will sweeten up. When among the leaders appear some great in heart and mind and absolutely free from self-seeking, their impact will be enough to make the crudities and crimes of the present age impossible."

We should expect our leaders to know their real nature, and in knowing their real nature, know reality. However great may be their leadership skills, abilities, achievements, all is worthless unless they are awake, unless they know their real nature and the nature of reality. This knowledge is the yeast that leavens all other leadership capabilities.

The leader I am describing is a transcendent leader. This new species of leader is defined by inner forces of consciousness, not by outer conditions of influence. The new species of leader is a lover of truth and a servant of reality. This new species is ordained by consciousness.

Transcendent leaders explore the true nature of self, mind, and reality. Their authority derives from this exploration. Such a leader's mind, heart, and conduct are all purified by silence. These leaders are scouts on the frontier of consciousness, adventuring into the wilderness of reality to open and clear the way, inviting and encouraging others to likewise explore.

We might want a set of criteria, a list of new species leadership skills, characteristics, and behaviors. Here is the list I would compose:

A rabbi, asked to define soul, said: "You know how when you're sleeping and you have a dream which you think is real, but then you wake up and see that the dream was just a dream; well, the soul is what we wake up into when we awaken from being awake." A leader is a person who, while being awake, wakes up a bit more.

Kabir, a 15th-century mystic, wrote, "When love hits the farthest edge of excess, it reaches wisdom. And the fragrance of that knowledge!" That fragrance is leadership.

The Buddhist monk Thich Nhat Hanh said, "The most basic precept of all is to be aware of what we do, what we are, each minute." This awareness is leadership.

The Tibetans have an adage, "Skillful means require insightful wisdom to produce effective action." Insightful wisdom is leadership.

The poet Rumi wrote, "A True Human Being is the essence, the original cause. The world and the universe are secondary effects." Leadership is the original cause.

The philosopher J. Krishnamurti said, "Between two thoughts there is a period of silence which is not related to the thought process." Leadership is that silence.

It will take some time for us to install such leaders within the hierarchies of our corporations and institutions. In the meantime, I suggest that every organization hire a mystic to serve as Vice President of Consciousness to help in the transition. These positions could be filled with such people as Huston Smith, Ram Dass, Thich Nhat Hanh, Marianne Williamson, Joanna Macy, Barbara Marx Hubbard, Caroline Myss, John Robbins, Stephen Levine, Jerry Jampolsky, Brother David Steindl-Rast, Jean Houston, Matthew Fox, Joseph Goldstein, Jack Kornfield, and Joan Borysenko.

These candidates seem sufficiently expert in matters of consciousness and conscience, courage and compassion, intelligence and wisdom to be the trustees of the transition from the old species of leader to the new. There are many, many more such qualified candidates, people who have spent years learning to read the wisdom scrolls that nature unfurls every evening in the amber twilight. Find them, hire them, learn from them. Let them tutor and inspire us. Let their current of deep living infiltrate every corner of our organizations. We shouldn't let our pride, arrogance, or vanity get in the way.

The mystic's mandate as a senior executive on the transition team—in addition to teaching the ways and means of mystical realization—is to challenge motives, question research, require accountability, insist upon the highest good. The other executives must listen and respond to them without turning away or stonewalling. These VPs would not be bound by corporate agreements of secrecy or oaths of loyalty. They would be free at any time to reveal the inner workings of the decision-making machinery. These VPs are monuments to awareness and truth, reminders of the spiritual world in which we live and work.

After years of meditation and contemplation on the true nature of self, mind, and reality, mystics will not get lost in the mind's hall-of-mirrors. They will not be seduced by the perks of power or swayed from a clear seeing of actions and consequences. They are to affirm the sacredness of life and assure that all activities are in compliance with such a sacred view. What does sacred mean? It refers to the mystical fact that everything is conscious, everything feels, thinks, and suffers. Everything is dependent upon everything else for its well-being, and everything is entitled to live and prosper in happiness and safety. The sacred view is to care for everything in the extreme. The sacred view does not exploit anything for profit, comfort, or convenience. When these mystic executives sense pollution or degradation, they know another way must be found. Their mandate is to safeguard the ecosystem of living beings, to promote awareness, to inspire compassionate action.

Please, let us do this. Let us embrace and enfold those among us who have dedicated their lives to awareness and consciousness. Let us admit that the old species of leader has failed us. Let us admit that we must quickly establish a regime of sacredness. As in all times of crisis, change, and transition, there will be protests and denials, difficulties and sorrow, sacrifice and loss. Let us trust captains of mysticism to help us navigate this turbulent time. They can show us how to turn our Earth-ship to the port or starboard and avoid the Titanic's fate.

Let us listen to the mystics who speak for the wisdom of our hearts, that we may find within us what we know but often forget, what we cherish but often disdain, what we love but often betray. Let our leaders be those among us who remember, and let us all remember so we may all become leaders.

For Personal Reflection

Think of a "transcendent leader" that you know or admire. Make a list of the qualities you admire in him or her. Now, imagine that person as the V.P. of Consciousness in your organization. How do you think other top executives would respond? In what ways do you think this vice president's influence would impact the way your organization does business? Spend some time imagining that you were given this role. How would you fulfill your responsibilities, according to the criteria in the chapter you've just read?

12

White House Voodoo

I think it is worth recalling and reflecting on the media brouhaha that occurred after Bob Woodward revealed in his book *The Choice* that Jean Houston had facilitated some visualizations for former First Lady Hillary Clinton.

Woodward mentions that the Clintons had invited a group of popular self-help authors, including Anthony Robbins, Marianne Williamson, and Stephen R. Covey, to Camp David. But it is Jean Houston—described as "an attractive woman with long, dark hair and a large, generous smile" wearing "an ancient Hellenistic coin of Athena set in a medallion around her neck all the time"—and her colleague Mary Catherine Bateson who receive most of Woodward's attention. Even so, the references are fairly brief.

These few paragraphs and Woodward's subsequent appearances on various television interview shows to promote the book lit a fire of interest seemingly out of proportion to the event. The media seized on the innocuous encounter between Houston and Clinton as though the Antichrist had suddenly appeared on the lawn of the White House. Over the course of several weeks, the firestorm of controversy generated numerous stories and media appearances by several of the protagonists of this drama. Talking heads pontificated endlessly. But the thing which needed to be said was never said.

I remember when Woodward spoke about his book with Stone Phillips on NBC's *Dateline*. The conversation turned to the matter of Jean Houston and her work with Hillary Clinton, and Phillips had the look of someone who had either just seen a ghost or glimpsed the Second Coming. He acted incredulous at what he was hearing. They did *what?* Woodward also seemed to enjoy the preposterousness of what had occurred.

In my own way, I was as incredulous as Phillips seemed to be, but not at Jean Houston and Hillary Clinton. I was incredulous at Phillips and Woodward, from whose reactions one would have thought that the First Lady had cavorted nude and mud-soaked under a full moon, instead of delighting in the very modest and rudimentary visualization techniques she actually practiced.

Their reactions reminded me of how reactionary much of our culture is in terms of awareness and reality, especially those sectors of society most in need of expanded consciousness: government, media, and business.

What was never said during the weeks of this story's media coverage was that such interest as Clinton's should be the norm. It should not be looked upon as some form of aberrant behavior. We should expect this and more from our leaders. We should expect them to be continually enhancing and expanding their awareness through spiritual development. This is unequivocally a prerequisite for leadership, just as it is for any intelligent, creative, effective, and truthful living. We must not follow, listen to, be influenced by, or in any way empower or legitimize any person who is not forging strong links to reality through meditation, self-inquiry, or other contemplative practices. Mystics must not be marginalized in society or defamed by those whose power is rooted in egoistic delusions and who, in the name of those delusions, serve only the specialized interests of power, greed, fear, and ignorance.

This is what was never said. No one took the accusers to task for their narrow-mindedness and ignorance. It seemed as though the Inquisition was back, in all its mad and misguided glory.

We are so hypnotized by the pettiness and frivolity of our consumer- and entertainment-based culture, so corrupted by the influence of money, power, and technology, so obsessed with celebrity and self-interest, so persuaded by politics and science, so victimized by sheer inattention and foolishness that many of us don't learn what must be learned until it is either almost too late, or too late. That is why we learn most in times of crisis, why we seem to awaken only in the presence of some catastrophic sadness. It is then that we are jolted out of our trance to see how puny and inconsequential our self-centered ideas, beliefs, and pursuits are.

We do not have time to tolerate the leadership of ignorance any longer. We must not allow any more Don Quixotes to decide our fate and the fate of our world, which is already teetering on the brink of preventable suicide. We must uplift, refine, and irradiate our consciousness with mystical understanding—right now, right this minute. If you are already doing this, if you are a true leader, a secret mystic, a closet ecstatic, a friend of reality, and a lover of truth, then you must come forward now. Please do not hide any longer. Please do not equivocate the truth of mysticism.

For Personal Reflection

Do you work in an environment in which contemplative practices would be ridiculed? If so, how does this affect you? Does the threat of peer or organizational judgment cause you to live a secret spiritual life? How does this feel? What steps might you consider taking at work to become more congruent with your inner life?

13

Seek Truth

A magazine publisher once asked me to write an article responding to his question: "What should a good leader think about?" I began that article by saying that leaders already think too much; they should stop thinking and seek truth. I said that leaders should give themselves totally, fully, and completely to the search for truth, without apology or embarrassment. They should become mystics—people who experience truth intuitively. All other leadership attributes, however important they may be, are secondary.

I would like to assume that all leaders are already fully committed to truth, reality, and consciousness. I would like to assume they know how to rely on awareness and intuition. I would like to assume they already know how to use thought judiciously, as a tool, and not abuse it nor be abused by it. But my assumptions are just that: my assumptions.

We must learn to seek truth all the time, seriously, deeply, profoundly—with our whole being. Seeking truth must become a second breath for us. We must breathe truth-seeking through the lungs that connect us to others, to the world, to the worlds beyond this world, to the invisible playgrounds of cosmic forces. These truth-seeking lungs are behemoth organs that oxygenate us with wisdom: our minds with clarity, our actions with integrity, our feelings with compassion.

I was recently advisor to a group of people who were growing their consulting and training company into an institute of broader scope and service capability. My role was to urge them to a deeper consideration of the issues we were discussing. At one point, we were scrutinizing a sentence contained in their values statement, trying to determine its underlying import and veracity. Finally, one participant blurted out, "It's time to put this to bed. This is just splitting hairs. The average person in the street will not notice these subtleties."

I responded, "But we are not asking these questions for the benefit of the average person on the street. We are asking them so we will know for ourselves what we are actually and truthfully intending to create. We are making the effort to become clear."

Still unconvinced, he replied, "Fine, but there is a time when you stop seeking truth and just get on with it."

I said, "Seeking the truth is getting on with it."

This person's response is not unusual. We can become impatient with continual questioning, irritable with prolonged examination of assumptions, angry at clarifying intentions and meanings. Though he knew in theory the value and importance of seeking the truth, he was reluctant to dive into it fully, to fully explore his own intentions. But we must do this if we are to truly know out of what fabric our motivations are woven, if we are to know what we are actually doing.

It is difficult to discipline ourselves to pay attention to the subtle underpinnings of our actions, those beliefs and assumptions which might distort our clear perception of what we are doing and how we are doing it. But we must pay attention to the quality of mind that is about to launch rocks into still ponds. We must know if there are lurking fears or secret ambitions that will cause our rocks to turn into missiles of sorrow.

So we must become patient, balanced, and calm, because a leader is a truth-seeker who never stops cultivating awareness, clarity, and truth.

What does seeking truth mean? It means to question everything with skillful, artistic persistence. It means that we always push against our certainty—of assumptions, knowledge, commitments, values, identities, and philosophies. To question is to seek truth, and leaders must ask questions that pertain to realms bigger than business. They must seek truth in territory larger than that defined by organization, product, market, pricing, manufacturing, and advertising. Truth-seeking questions are profoundly beautiful and soul-stunning in their implications. Here are some truth-seeking questions: Who am I? What am I doing? Why am I doing it? How am I doing it? Who will benefit? Who will be harmed? What might be the consequences of my actions upon generations yet to come? What are beliefs and what do I believe? How are beliefs different from reality? What is real? What is power? What is death? From where does the fire in the belly of my ambitions come? Why do I react the way I do? Can one really achieve security? What is success? What is money and its right use? What does freedom mean? What is love?

In questioning, go deep. Develop stamina. Practice. Become resilient, strong, unwavering, and implacable. Become a genius of questioning. In seeking truth, explore everything. Seeking truth is potent, and it keeps us flexible, fluid, and free, lithe figures dancing in beautiful constellations of incomparable symmetry, permeable by life's infinite mystery and beauty.

A leader is one who wears the crown of life's mystery and beauty, bestowed by that inner truth sought for and found, again and again.

For Personal Reflection

Do you regularly examine your assumptions to see how valid they are? Do you become impatient or angry when your beliefs are challenged? Are you willing to take the time to seek deeper levels of truth, especially at work, especially when you are expected to produce results quickly? Make a list of at least ten benefits to seeking truth. Make a list of the reasons why you don't seek truth. Compare the lists. What are you willing to do?

14

Epiphanies

Transcendent leaders love epiphanies, sudden monsoons of intuitive perception, revelatory manifestations of clear awareness, direct knowledge of the nature of reality. Epiphanies disturb our cherished assumptions and beliefs about life and disrupt our conditioned, mechanical patterns of behavior.

Epiphanies come to us through a variety of means: intentional practice, an accident, a sudden reversal of fortune, the death of a loved one, a confrontation with our own mortality, or by divine grace. Another way in which epiphanies may appear in our lives is through an encounter with a mystic, a living conduit of pure consciousness.

I experienced an epiphany of this last kind a few years ago at the Mt. Madonna Center in Watsonville, California. It is a retreat facility founded by Baba Hari Dass, an Indian yogi who has not spoken a word since 1952. I was facilitating a planning session for the management team of a computer chip manufacturing company. I had arranged a private meeting with our group and Baba Hari Dass, who communicates succinctly and humorously by writing on a chalkboard. We visited with him for about 30 minutes, asking a variety of questions, including several about spirituality in business. When our time was over, I went to thank him. A force emanated from his eyes that I had experienced in the eyes of my teacher many years earlier. It was a ray that could penetrate very deeply into the core of one's being: it was the touch of reality, or grace, that causes one to awaken to another world of significance.

As I walked outside with our group, I suddenly felt very strange, light-headed, and off balance. I told my associate to continue without me, and that I would catch up. I wandered into a grove of trees, found a boulder, and sat down. Something pierced my heart. I bent over and started crying. It's very hard to say what occurred to me then. It is probably difficult for all of us to speak of these moments—so full of silence and beauty and awakening.

When I stopped crying, I sat still for a long time. Everything about me seemed newly alive and radiant, as though I was seeing these common things for the first time: flowers, trees, rocks, and dirt. It seemed that everything was breathing! I felt light and spacious, extending beyond the familiar boundary of my body. I became aware of an orderly connection between things, much as when you finally piece a puzzle together and see how each piece fits into the other to form the whole. I was relieved of a burden I didn't know I was carrying. I was embraced by a profound peace.

When these disruptions to our conventional way of living occur, it's as though we see another dimension of life about which we were ignorant. The mask of appearance falls away, and we see something profound about life. We experience something of the timeless, the real, that which gives radiance to us in the womb. It's beyond words, and the mind hardly grasps it. In these moments, the fortifications against the soul dissolve, and a new perspective appears.

A client of mine, the president of a high-tech company in Silicon Valley, told me the real reason he goes fly-fishing in the Sierras. He didn't particularly care for fishing, but he said it was an acceptable excuse to stand all day thigh-deep in the comforting current of a mountain stream, surrounded by trees, rocks and clouds, stillness and silence, finding peace while learning the dialects of nature.

He loses himself while standing in the streams of the Sierras. The beauty and silence of nature draw out his soul and liberate him from the anxiety and pressures of life.

He says that the top of his head opens and something of him flies up and out and finally hooks in the mouth of a fish swimming in eternity. He says he disappears into a peace that he can't really describe in which everything seems to sparkle. Is this not an epiphany?

And yet he could not directly face this, could not directly admit his yearning for this communion. He pretended to love fly-fishing. He couldn't just admit that he hiked into the mountains to feel his soul and connection to fish swimming in eternity.

Many of us are secretive about our longing to unite with the larger beauty of which we are a part. Why are we embarrassed to admit that we want to live in this pristine wilderness of spiritual communion?

What impact might this man have if he would return to the office with the billowing clouds of his soul tied to a string wrapped around a finger so as not to forget? Sitting at his desk in his office, wouldn't he be as open as the mountain skies, as patient as the trees, as articulate as the stream? To touch him would be to feel the pulse of that gorgeous and picturesque consciousness that imbues the streams in the Sierras with unending delight and silence.

Leaders should gorge on silence. Leaders should love inspiring collisions with the spirit; they should welcome mystical perceptions with wild abandon. Leaders should learn how to play the furious and wordless jazz of that silence which blows life into all things.

Let us be taken by silence into that vital part of ourselves, perhaps forgotten, perhaps ignored, but compelling beyond reason. The living wholeness of our Self is found in silence, and silence should be the language of leaders.

Let this silence and this love of the Self affect us, take us, overwhelm us. Let us give ourselves to this as to music, to reverie, to beauty. Let the silence that we are create a cataclysm of clarity in our lives.

Let our doubts and confusion meet this living wholeness. Let our rage and torment meet this living wholeness. Let our unquenchable cravings meet this living wholeness. Let our efforts to bring peace into our lives and into the world meet this living wholeness, the sacred Self of all whose name is love, creator of the universe.

The supreme silence, the primordial essence, the breathing spirit is crawling at warp speed through every tree's sap-channel and through every lovely child's mystery; it shapes the calls of wild dogs, and blesses the collapse of stars as they sip their own mortality. Let us celebrate and remember that we are that silence.

For Personal Reflection

Allow yourself a few minutes of quiet. Sit or lie in a comfortable position. Let your awareness open to a time when you experienced an epiphany, a sudden experience of union with life or an insight into the nature of reality. Let the remembrance of this epiphany come fully into your awareness.

What does this experience tell you about your life? What conflicts do you experience between what the epiphany teaches and how you actually live? Are you open with others about these kinds of experiences? If not, why? How would your life be different if you allowed the insight of an epiphany to shape and guide your life?

15

Weird Failures

The doors to the invisible world of our soul often close early, when we are inoculated against its wildness by the forces of convention. From the time the doors close, we live on in a deathly darkness, like those poor souls in Plato's cave who were chained to the ground, facing the cave-walls. They could see only the dim and smoky figures created by the fire, and believed them to be the sum total of reality. Every so often, a daring person would manage to break free and find freedom, where the real world would crash upon them like a tidal wave of joy. They'd return to the others, but none would believe their stunning reports. People become leaders when they break free from the chains of ignorance and dive into the tidal waves of joy, when they smash open the darkening doors that have been shuttered and locked, inhibiting the soul from bursting out.

One day at an airport, I was reminded of how the doors close upon the daring freedom of the soul's passions and exuberance, of how we get into trouble for singing aloud the songs of the mystical world. In the lounge, waiting for the boarding call, was a young girl of about three, maybe four years old. She had a glorious bright look. Energy and enthusiasm would rise within her like giant waves. Her life welled up from deep within her, unconditioned and unafraid, raw and vital. It was beautiful. Waves of great soul force shook her with tenderness. She must have dreamed beautiful dreams. I am sure she knew the blessings of her mystical ancestors and played with subtle beings from other dimensions, just as many of us did before we were reprimanded by the call of the fierce world. Her doors were wide open.

"Jennifer, come here!" said her mother. She wasn't angry, just distracted, but her tone was sharp, and became sharper, with a hint of punishment. She seemed like a good person who was simply distressed by her daughter's tidal waves of joy. Nonetheless, a door slammed shut within the little girl.

"Don't do that!" Another door closed.

Then another. "Be careful."

Another. "Be quiet."

"Stand still."

"Don't bother people."

Within five minutes, so many doors closed that I wondered how the poor girl would ever open them all again: *stay here, be good, don't fidget, be quiet, be careful, come back here, don't do that, don't touch that, stand still, listen to what I tell you, don't make me angry.*

This isn't just an insignificant anecdote. It has happened to all of us. The mother's commands hit the little girl with forbidding force, a punch of fear and dread. The girl's little body froze with each command, shocked and traumatized. With each trauma, her subconscious mind seemed to whir and decide: I will never do *this* again. The little girl did not need to be physically hit to be hurt, to be cut by the authoritative commands. Within the subterranean processes of her thoughts and feelings, she decided it was not a good idea to anger her meal ticket of security, love, and approval.

This is what happens. Once we begin, there is no end to the turning away. With each humiliation, with each embarrassment, with each shocking abuse, we decide, and those decisions become festering wounds. With each decision, we shape and mold ourselves into a form, an ego, a pattern of identity and response based on a suppression of our inner life and its impulses. We turn from radiance to darkness, from joy to sorrow, from depth to shallowness—each turn creating momentum, until we become permanently disfigured: dizzy and confused, fearful and ashamed, obedient and numb.

These closing doors separate us from our natural exuberance, our unique expression of the creative life force. We turn against our own enthusiasm, wonder, awe, curiosity, playfulness, and connectedness to others. As the doors close, we become diminished in spiritual clarity and capacity. We suppress and deny those tidal waves of spontaneous energy, enthusiasm, and joy because we learn they may jeopardize our safety, security, and acceptance. Many of us have not yet unlearned that lesson, but we must. This is the inner work that leaders must do.

With the first blow, the first bruise, we begin to take our instructions from outside, from others. We start taking notes on what is permissible, what is appropriate. We fill mental note pads with the authoritative teachings of those who have come before us, who themselves learned and now teach that only the dirty, smoky figures on the cave wall are real. We become inoculated against our own inner force, and day by day we lose our luster and light. Like cheetahs and gazelles, we are stolen away from the natural veldts of our true home and put in crates, cement-block cells, and display cases. Our self-betrayal begins here, when we believe without question what we are told, when we begin to obey and turn from our own radiance. It can begin even on our very first day in the world.

One of my clients experienced regular emotional upsets, which translated into frequent breakdowns of his work commitments. He asked me to work with him, to help him find out why he lived in such a way.

It didn't take long, because he was ready to change. He broke free during a period of meditation and deep breathing which returned him to the moment of his birth. He remembered his mother's disappointment that her child was a boy, and she said to the doctor, "I don't want to hold him. I wanted a girl. Take him away."

His mother was not greatly interested in him, and he had to learn techniques and tactics to attract her attention and love. He did that by creating upsets and breakdowns in his young life. The attention he got, though it was often negative and harsh, was better than nothing. He thought this attention was love. He drew negative attention to himself, confusing that with love. This pattern of attracting attention, "love," sank into the depths of his subconscious mind. He continued to enact this pattern throughout his life, without knowing why. Until his breakthrough.

My client began to separate himself from his mother's comment. He no longer used it as the basis of his self-image. He was able to glimpse who he was before all this distortion and awkwardness. He began to see his original face, as the grit and grime were cleaned from his eyes.

I worked with a very successful businessman who thought he was without a soul. He had refused a missionary assignment from his church and had subsequently been excommunicated. He was told that the church would repossess his soul, and he would live out his life bereft of God's love and grace. My client believed the church and lived accordingly.

I can't remember seeing anyone so uptight, nervous, and edgy. On the one hand, he behaved like an existentialist mob boss, stepping hard on everyone, pushing his way to the front of every line to grab more than his share. Why not? *If I can't get into God's heaven and experience eternal heavenly delights, then I'm for goddamn sure going to get everything I can, here and now.*

On the other hand, something inside him did not believe his church. He told me, "I've got everything. But it's killing me. Living this way . . . it's killing me. Even if God has forsaken me, I haven't forsaken God."

With that realization, he broke free and was swept up by a tidal wave of joy. Later, we designed a ritual so he could repossess his soul from his church. He, too, found his original face in the mirror of his own heart, as clean and bright as it was on the first day of creation.

Most of my consulting work is about these weird failures. That is not, of course, my clients' initial request, which is usually about some collapse of leadership or breakdown of personal or team communication and performance. In truth, their problems are always about their weird failures, projected into the world without their conscious knowledge.

The external world of weird failures is the reflection of our inner discord, a picture of our hurt, pain, fear, and anger. This is what Kabir is referring to in his poem: *The truth is, you turned away yourself, and decided to go into the dark alone. You've forgotten what you once knew; that's why everything you do has some weird failure in it.* Leaders know this and dedicate themselves to restoring themselves to their spiritual essence, so that the spiritual essence can become realized in the reflective neutrality of the world-canvas.

I was meeting with a client who was a corporate president, to prepare for a senior management team retreat on organizational effectiveness. We had just reviewed my summary of interviews with his executive team, and the feedback about his leadership had brought our conversation to a pause. Some of what people had to say was flecked with anger, disappointment, and frustration. I had presented it as it was told to me, and I also tried to transmit the emotional energy of the senior team members. He was shaken.

After some silence, we resumed our conversation, and my client turned from business matters to extremely personal ones. He explosively defended himself against what he perceived to be a personal attack, in the face of which he felt betrayed and unappreciated.

He leaned forward in his chair, shaking with emotion. "When they need help, don't I take care of them? Don't I help them? When they make mistakes, don't I forgive them? But who forgives me? Who helps me? Who will take care of me? Who will love me?"

I remained silent while he wept. I had seen him approach this threshold before, but not cross it. Now that he had, the real issues were clear, and they had nothing to do with the company or his leadership. The issues were sadness, despair, loneliness, and fear. These are often the real concerns everywhere, and the problems we want to fix are just symptoms of these more elemental issues, the weird failure of forgetting what we once knew.

We externalize these failures and then try to solve the problems. The problems remain. No one really knows what to do. The more we try to solve the problems, the more the weird failures seem to proliferate. The weird failures are symptoms of turning from our radiant soul toward a world of forgetfulness. This is what Kabir was talking about. There is something we have all forgotten, and that forgetfulness makes us heavy and sad. It makes us anxious, fearful, and angry. The weird failures have to do with forgetting who we are, with turning away from the spirit which gives us radiance. This alienation causes us to suffer, and we act out that suffering in the world. The world's chaotic and brutal throes are our screams of alienation and forgetfulness. The chaos in the world persists because we have not yet faced ourselves with the sincere intent to heal and become whole again.

"Each of us must be the change we want to see in the world," said Gandhi. In order to be the change we want to see in the world, we must look deeply inward and know ourselves as we are, in our essence. This knowledge will put an end to the chaos.

People whose weird failures are not healed inevitably re-create their pain as tragic world events. They will create the preconditions for these tragedies, because they cannot create the preconditions for peace, justice, and harmony. They do not know these for themselves. Wherever there is abuse of power, fraud, corruption, violence, lies, deception, and repression of freedom, know that there is soullessness. The history of war is the history of soullessness.

This is why we need leaders who will return to their original radiance.

Leaders have to reclaim their souls, and to do so they will have to enter themselves deeply in order to heal and forgive. In order to reclaim the radiance from which they have turned, they must understand how their beauty is pummeled and how they become alienated from their souls. They must understand how soul alienation corrupts their minds with fear and anger, and how those emotions become their calling cards. They cannot live in their reasons and justifications: those are only masks. If they remain the puppets of buried decisions, how can they ever create new behavior, new solutions?

Only leaders who heal their pain and anger will be able to precondition the world for inspiring, life-affirming, unifying world events.

Until we understand our own weird failures, we are nothing but terrorists to ourselves and others, brutalizing the world to compensate for soullessness. Without the deep feeling and awareness of what life is, of what we are in our original nature, there can be no love, no joy, and no peace in this world. We will seek compensation from the world for the dents to our soul, the blows to our heart. We can never be sufficiently compensated. We cannot make the world pay for our spiritual loss. We must recover for ourselves what was "lost." We must look to where our lost soul still lives, waiting to be found again. We must find each dent, each bruise, each decision, and heal each one with the light touch of love, compassion, and understanding.

For Personal Reflection

Are you the aware of decisions you have made in the past that continue to direct your behavior without your knowing it? Are unresolved emotional hurts or disappointments interfering in your life in destructive ways? What steps can you take to reduce the number of weird failures in your life?

16
Shooting Galleries

It is easy to see the pockmarked, desperate face of addiction in crack houses and heroin shooting galleries in the devastated Dresdens of America's inner cities. It is not so easy to see the same depleted face in the mirror of addictions to ideas, power, wealth, celebrity, work, religion, anger, self-pity, and possessions. But these are every bit as mean and corrosive to our spirit and to our soul as are crack, heroin, and hopelessness.

An addiction refers to anything we do or use habitually to provide a sense of well-being. Often we are not even aware that we have an addiction. We think we are always in control, that we can do or not do, use or not use as we choose. This is not the case. Very few of us are free from addictions. In fact, most of us are defined by addictions we don't even know we have. We can't give them up because we have become our addictions. We hardly know who we are without them.

Leaders will have to face their addictions and overcome them. They will have to pass through the trials of withdrawal in order to become free. Freedom and reality are mirror and image, image and mirror. Where there is reality, there is freedom; where there is freedom, there is reality. This is all that is necessary for well-being.

Actor Charles Grodin once said during his talk show that the media will do anything for a good story. Heroin addicts will do anything for a good fix. They are incapable of being responsible and evaluating the consequences of their actions. Heroin addicts are not free. They cannot choose, cannot do the right thing, cannot see anything in perspective, cannot be generous and kind. Heroin addicts act compulsively. They cannot sit quietly in deep meditation until the true action comes about from silence, from reality. Heroin addicts cannot be trusted; we know they will do anything for their next fix. They are not creative, compassionate, intelligent, intuitive, just, truthful, or accountable. They cannot contribute meaning, beauty, and significance to themselves, others, society, or the world.

Can we say that we are not an addict until we acknowledge our own addictions? Many of us may be just like the heroin addicts, although our addictions may be socially sanctioned, and therefore invisible.

Are people in the media addicted to a "good story"? Can they turn from a story if their conscience, if their soul, tells them to? This is a serious issue for leaders. Leaders must be free, addicted to nothing, serenely detached. Leaders must be free to be used by reality, not by their addictions. Leaders will not depend upon anything other than reality for their well-being, for their identity, for their purpose, for their welfare. Leaders will never be compromised by money, celebrity, fame, power, vengeance, pride, arrogance, vanity, anger, or jealousy. Leaders, unlike addicts, are never compulsive, hurtful, deceitful, and destructive. Leaders will not rely on artificial means for their highs in life. Leaders must be willing to recover their freedom from any addictions or cravings of insufficiency they may have.

A leader's belly is full, a leader's heart is at peace, a leader's mind is content—all from loving reality.

We may think of dependency in terms of substances or relationships. But let's look deeper. What happens when we can't watch our favorite television program, when the morning paper isn't delivered, or the hot water heater breaks? How agitated do we become during a power failure, or when the lights, computers, and phones stop working?

Do we view our normal expectations as addictions? If the test of addiction is the trauma of deprivation, can we face the enormity of our addictions? What about our very life? When we contemplate our death, do we do so serenely, with understanding and openness? If one is sincerely trying to live freely, creatively, we must wonder about all of this, and try to find out if we can live without the trauma of deprivation stalking us from the shadow of our craving.

We are propped up in a hundred ways that we don't notice. We are addicted to our view of reality. We are addicted to our religious beliefs, without which we would be lost. Our identities, roles, and beliefs are all addictions, aren't they? Can we give everything up and be free? Are we not addicted to having our own way, to imposing our will on events? Are we not addicted to our past?

If we look at addiction in this larger view, who is not an addict? Is a politician not addicted to power? Is an evangelist not addicted to rhetoric? Is a scientist not addicted to proof? Is a businessperson not addicted to profit?

It is a shock to see our own addictions. If everything we depend on were taken away, who would we be? Are we not addicted to our own self-centeredness? Are we not dependent on the events of our lives to give us a sense of coherence and meaning? Are we not addicted to thinking, to projecting our fears, anxieties, hopes, and wishes into the future? Don't we look to our accomplishments for a sense of pride? Can we live without this? Let's be honest, and look precisely at the whole issue of addiction, how we depend on something to keep us intact.

An addict will do anything for the next fix. Will we? How much hostility, violence, and greed do we rationalize in the name of our unexamined addictions? An addict will do anything. Isn't so much of our own compulsive, chaotic existence manufactured by our addictions?

Sitting silently, can we see the first impulse of craving? It takes courage and honesty to see our whole predicament, but we must do so in order to be free. We fight so hard for freedom from external oppression, should we not want to be equally free from internal oppression, from the slavery of compulsion and craving?

When we experience a moment when craving is absent, we will understand addiction and what to do about it. Have you ever sat in a forest at night, unafraid, bathed in moonlight, listening to the Earth's breathing and the leaves dancing on the hard ground? Something opens within us, and this opening is both empty and solid at the same time. Profound stillness of mind. A quivering in the heart of what is wordlessly present. In this depth of being, without movement, utterly still, is a total absence of craving and dependence. Returning to silence, to our source, reveals our wholeness, and in wholeness we become free.

Have we ever experienced a moment of true freedom? Have we ever experienced freedom from addiction?

In a moment of awakening, of experiencing our innate wholeness, craving disappears. There is no other thing to depend on, no other place to go, no other time to covet, no condition to medicate or escape, no hole to fill. In this awakening to wholeness is simplicity, the joy of everyday life, the acceptance of everyday thoughts and feelings. No need to run, no need to hide, no need to fear, no need to crave. Simplicity is openness and wonder, simplicity is peace. Peace is who we are. When we know who we are, we are free: this freedom dissolves the condition that is the root of all cravings, attachments, and dependent identifications.

Leaders must become free of addictions.

For Personal Reflection

For the next two weeks, take only cold showers. How do you respond to the lack of hot water? Make a list of at least ten things you are accustomed to. For example, the plentiful supply of gas at your local gas station. What would happen to you if you were suddenly deprived of them? Spend some time reflecting on your reactions to this deprivation. What do your reactions tell you about the ways in which your well-being is determined by your dependencies?

Do these dependencies determine your inner state of well-being? Do these dependencies determine your choices and decisions, your priorities and goals?

How dependent are you on your beliefs, your self-image, your status in society?

What does freedom from addiction mean for you?

17

The American Dream

The American Dream is an ideal of life based on personal financial success. The American Dream is about getting all the marbles that the material world has to offer. How we do it is not important. What is important is that we get the marbles. If we go through life with no marbles, or only four or five marbles, we will have lost the game of life. If we get all the marbles, or a lot of them, then we will have won the game of life. This is the American Dream.

The American Dream is really the American Nightmare.

The Dream confuses the worth of something in the marketplace of the physical world with its significance in the spiritual world of the soul. The premise of the Dream is based on a misperception about life. The essence of life, its lungs and heart and soul, lies in the invisible, spiritual world. The American Dream is about money, whereas life is about significance. This is why so many people who have planted their flags on summits of personal achievement and success are still empty, soulless, and desperate. If the marketplace worth of something does not originate in the soul's invisible world, it will have no significance, and therefore it will never feed us, it will never fill our hungry bellies.

In 1941, Victor Ganz bought Pablo Picasso's painting *The Dream* for seven thousand dollars. In 1997 he sold it for 48.4 million dollars. The worth of the painting had increased unimaginably.

Its worth, however, has nothing to do with significance. The Mecca of our society is cash. We value making money above all else. We love, admire, and celebrate cash cows. Our society demonstrates other values, to be sure, but these aren't as dominant as our love of making money. Our inordinate love of money is disconnected from the significance of the invisible world of our soul. If you doubt this, spend a day in a trading pit. It is in these pits that the true religion of our culture is practiced: fast cash.

Money can be a servant or a master, a means or an end. In the American Dream, money is the master. Making money has become an end in and of itself. In our *koyaanisqatsi* culture, money has become the sole criterion for success, significance, goodness, and truth. Our love of money has blinded us.

Leaders will know that money is a means, not an end. Leaders will make money serve the significance of the soul, and will make money serving the true needs of people, not those spurious needs trumped up by their own marketing departments.

The only time I ever saw my elder brother cry was shortly after our father died. Family and friends had gathered at our house to comfort one another. I noticed my brother wander out to the back yard and then slip through the gate into the neighboring park. After a while, I went out and joined him. He was sitting cross-legged on the dirty grass, head down, sobbing. I don't remember specifically what we spoke of, but I know it had something to do with the deep feelings for life and for those we love which reveal themselves after a great loss.

I know that something was said about taking time to smell the roses, about loving, about being present with people instead of living on the freeways of our future hopes and aspirations. I remember rhetorical questions like, "What the hell have I been doing?" Something was said about touching deeper, connecting, feeling, loving, and appreciating life itself. I'm sure we spoke of what people everywhere speak of when a father, mother, wife, husband, or child dies suddenly and unexpectedly—and we realize too late that there was something we wanted to say, but didn't; something we wanted to do, but didn't; some way we wanted to be, but weren't. In speaking together after death's rude intrusion, we discover something universal about life, and significance.

Death is a great teacher which can awaken and enlighten us. Death's teaching power comes from its relationship to life, the cycles of life, the laws of life: everything is impermanent, everything is born, grows, ages, and dies. We don't know if that cycle will last one hour, 100 years or 10,000 years. Death teaches us that we are not in control, that there are greater, invisible forces than us at work in the universe. Death teaches us about now, about this moment, because we realize that it may be our last moment.

Seeing the naked face of our last moment is like falling into an icy stream. We come to full attention very quickly. We instantly forget what is inessential, and remember what is essential. The mystical experience is also an icy stream, and plunging into its breathtaking waters shocks us into significance.

When we are awake to what truly has significance, we lose our lust for what merely has value in the marketplace. I am not speaking against prosperity and abundance. I am speaking for the kind of prosperity and abundance that is often forgotten, trampled, and betrayed in our quest for money before all else.

One of my clients was the chief financial officer of a project management company. He was twenty-seven years old, married, and the father of an infant son. He was hard on others, impatient and unforgiving. He was even harder on himself. In one of our first meetings, he outlined his plans and goals: he wanted to retire in ten years, with plenty of marbles. That is when he would relax; until then he had to press hard on the grindstone. His wife, who also worked full-time, would bring their son with her to my client's office on Saturdays and Sundays: it was the only way she could see him. They had agreed this was the time to work hard, earn money, and get ahead.

One day I received a call. "Rob, two nights ago I burned myself when I was cooking dinner. Not too badly, but I went to the ER anyway. They took a routine blood test. Today I got the results. I have leukemia."

His plans changed.

I offered what support I could. I introduced him to relaxation, meditation and visualization techniques, and to the books and tapes of Bernie Siegel and others who speak about the mind/body connection and about the spiritual dimension to healing. We began to speak in depth about things we had only spoken of briefly at the office: values, life and its meaning, plans and their elusiveness, control and surrender, personal will and a higher power. He began to review his life and previous goals in light of these reflections.

At one point during his subsequent chemotherapy, his weight dropped from 255 pounds to about 145. He was six feet four inches tall. At that time, the prognosis was not favorable.

On one of my visits to the hospital, I asked him if he had thought about his death.

A little.

Would you like to speak about that?

Yes.

We didn't speak about death, but about life.

I screwed up. I've been chasing the wrong things. I never took the time to appreciate what I really value.

What do you value?

My wife. My kid. I've hardly noticed them. My God, I value just being alive. I've spent my whole life trying to buy a boat while my life raced by. Now, it might be over and I haven't even lived it.

Why do we so often wait until it is late, or too late, to awaken to a life of significance?

Almost ten years ago, I was asked by one of my clients, a corporate president, to design a values retreat for his executive team.

Seven of us set out on horseback and trotted off into the Santa Cruz Mountains like urban gunfighters on a mission. We made camp beneath ancient redwoods. The first day we settled in, exhaling the tension, congestion, noise, and complexity of the city. I wanted the presence, silence, and antiquity of the forest to enter us, individually and as a group, before we started our work.

The next day, we began. I said that any group values statement had to come from individual values statements. If what we, as a group, are going to say is important, then it had better be important to each of us. We can't fake values, I said. I led the seven through a visualization, to get them in touch with the most significant experience they could remember. I thought that would be a good place to begin by having each one speak about what they valued: go to a valuable experience and mine it.

I asked each person to describe the experience that came to them during the meditation, and what that experience taught them about significance. A vice-president, in his mid-fifties and a former Marine Corps pilot, told of how, when he was 15, he was suddenly transported out of his body. He experienced himself as pure light and was intensely joyful. He felt that he was actually a part of all living things. He said, struggling for the words and with soft tears forming in his eyes, that this light body was the body of everything and that love was the universal spirit of life, binding all living things together as one. He said he experienced himself as this love, and that he existed everywhere. He said it was an experience that was thrilling beyond words.

He said it was the most significant experience of his life, though he had not spoken of it for over 40 years. He sat quietly for a bit, and then he said that he didn't feel anyone would understand. He himself didn't understand. There was no support for that experience. He felt it was an anomaly of some kind and thought it best to forget about it. He hadn't known how to build his life from this most significant experience.

Leaders will know the difference between money and significance. Leaders will know that money is a servant, the means of something greater than itself. Leaders will not inflame the unquenchable desires of people for the sake of profit. Leaders will have spoken with their own death. They will be well aware and awake within the eternal world of soul. Leaders will be as strong a teacher as death. Leaders will be stern but loving teachers of significance. Leaders will help us calibrate our relationship to money by inflaming our souls, by touching our hearts, and by reminding us of what life is.

Leaders will know that we must awaken from all dreams and nightmares to live in accord with reality. Reality is a leader's value, a leader's fragrance, a leader's behavior. Leaders are prophets of the soul's transcendent world of beauty, love, and joy. Leaders are servants of the soul.

For Personal Reflection

How much of your life is devoted to earning money? Do you do this in a way that nourishes your inner life? Have you ever betrayed your inner life for the sake of money? What were the consequences? Was it worth it? Do you feel that your relationship to money is governed by your highest knowing about life?

18

Walking the Talk

A few years ago, I was asked by the owner of a communications company to evaluate the degree to which his company expressed their corporate values in day-to-day activities and interactions.

He asked me if I wanted to review their corporate values documents. I said no. He asked if I would circulate a survey or questionnaire. I said no. He asked if I would use some form of assessment tool. I said no. He asked if I wanted to interview people one-on-one, or in small groups. I said no, I don't want to talk to anyone.

He asked how I was going to proceed. I said that I was going to use my mute button assessment tool, and that I was going to stuff cotton in my ears and then just walk around watching people work for three days. After that, I would be able to tell him what their actual values were, based on how people conducted themselves in the course of their work. I told him that I would rather observe how his people acted and in so doing get to know them as they really are, not as he or they like to think they are. I told him I would rather watch them—without any explanation—to see how they interacted with themselves and each other, with customers, vendors, suppliers, the public, OSHA, and the fire department.

That is the true values document: how people behave. If people don't like their behavior, they can change. But they have to see how they actually behave: those are their values-in-action, which are the only values worth paying attention to. To superimpose a set of idealized behaviors on top of our actual behavior is a sure way to institutionalize hypocrisy.

I never listen to anyone speak about their values. I'd rather watch them. The truth is, we are always expressing our values. We might think that our real values are what we say they are, but that is a delusional conceit. Our real values are expressed in our actions, in what we do and how we do it. Our actions never contradict our values. Our actions *are* our values.

If we believe our values are what we say they are, then we will also believe all the reasons and excuses we give about why we don't live up to them. The simple reason we don't live up to our espoused values is that they are not our actual values. "People are our greatest asset" is a popular espoused value of the corporate sector. Though this value is declared, spoken, and repeated by thousands of people every day, we can scarcely see the demonstration of it. It isn't that we fall short because of this devil or that reason. We fall short because we do not value people as our greatest asset.

If we want to know what we value, then we have only to watch what we do and how we do it. If we don't like what we see about ourselves as we observe this, then we can change our behavior.

We don't need to refer to any papers or books or stone tablets for our values. Doing so creates unnecessary tension and anxiety, which further obscures what we actually do. We act from what we are, from what is written on the tablet of our hearts. If there is some values work to be done, it is in our own hearts. We need to change who we are from the inside out, not because someone else says we should, but because we have looked into the mirror of our actual behavior and we don't like what we see.

I was asked by the president of a small R&D company to help them develop a set of values which would help guide their imminent growth. During our first meeting, he spoke about the company's history and outlined their mission and current goals. We spoke about some of the tensions and problems he hoped to alleviate by creating a clear set of values.

I asked him what he valued more than anything else.

He asked for clarification.

I asked him to tell me what he valued more than anything else in life. I asked him to name that single thing which made his life go.

He got up and closed the door to his office. When he sat down, he asked me if I meant at work or in general.

I said there was no difference. There was only life.

After a while, he said that he thought the most important thing in life was love.

I asked him how many people were on his executive team.

He said eight, and that most of them had been with him for about five years.

I remarked that probably all eight of those people knew that love was his most important value.

He said probably not.

I said six.

He said no.

Five?

No.

I asked, "Well, how many of these people with whom you have worked 10 hours a day, five days a week, for five years, would know that love is your most important value?"

He hesitated, and then he said, "Probably none."

If that was true, I said, then he was lying about love being his most cherished value, because if it were, everyone would know it.

For Personal Reflection

Make a list of the top five values which you feel guide your life and work. Do they? If not, why? What reasons do you give for not acting from what you say you value? Can you see that whenever you act, you act from what you value in that moment and in that situation? Can you see that your values are always expressed in your actions? What are the implications of this for you?

19

All Things Are Sentient

If we were to become sensitized to reality, we would no longer objectify other living things. We would begin to feel their feelings, intuit their language and meanings, and understand their rightful place in the world. We would come to know that all things are sentient, that "animate" and "inanimate" are false distinctions. We would become very discreet about interfering with, abusing, killing, and destroying other living creatures. We would become very careful about polluting and defiling the Earth and her lakes, rivers, oceans, and atmosphere. We would, as the Buddha said, see ourselves in others, and thus cause them no harm.

We do not act as though we know all things are sentient. As it is now, we act like madmen who want to purge the Earth of her forests, plants, and animals, strip her of topsoil, pollute every stream, lake, and ocean, defile her air, and push nuclear waste deep into her living center. We do this as though it were our supreme mission in life. We do this in the name of economic growth, personal prosperity, and divine right. This is insanity.

The Earth loses about 50 million acres of rain forests a year, endangering hundreds of species of trees, plants, mammals, birds, reptiles, amphibians, and insects. Today, global biological diversity faces a rate of species destruction greater than at any time since the mass extinction of the dinosaurs 65 million years ago.

The systemic desecration of the Earth and her inhabitants is occurring. We are doing it, or we are allowing it to happen. We are behaving as though someone challenged us, "See if you can make the Earth uninhabitable within 50 years. Ready, set, go!" Why are we not ashamed of our behavior?

We can only act in this way if we do not feel the sentience of all living things. If we did, we simply could not do what we do. We would feel the pain and suffering of the world's creatures as keenly as we would the mutilation of our own children.

We have all suffered. We have all experienced pain, fear, loss, and hurt. We are grateful to anyone who helps us heal our pain and relieve our suffering. We are grateful to anyone who shows us compassion. We are grateful for the touch of kindness, for the caress of love. Compassion and love elevate our life to the realm of the sacred. Everything is sacred. Everything deserves our respect, our compassion, and our love. Everything.

If we could truly feel another's suffering, we would respond with love. No other response is adequate. No other response is appropriate. Finding love within ourselves, we see it everywhere, for we are not different from other living beings and creatures. We are one with them. Their suffering is ours. Their pain is ours. Their fear is ours. Feeling this, we can only respond with compassion, kindness, and love.

Leaders will know that all things are sacred. They will serve all living beings with compassion, kindness, and love.

Vivisection is animal experimentation—burning, shocking, drugging, starving, scalding, irradiating, blinding, and killing animals. According to PETA, People for the Ethical Treatment of Animals, each year in the United States an estimated 70 million animals are so treated in the name of science, by private institutions, household product and cosmetics companies, government agencies, educational institutions, and scientific centers.

As a society, we have created animal death camps, where millions of animals live in a Dachau or Auschwitz, where they are subjected to horrendous tortures and mutilations. Why can we not hear their screams?

We cut, stab, splay, flay, starve, irradiate, inflame, poison, and kill millions of animals every year. How is it that we cannot feel their pain and suffering?

Would we bring our own young children into these labs? Would we ask our lovely young daughters and sons to come in on a Sunday, perhaps after some religious outing, to sew closed the eyes of monkeys, or to set a pig on fire, or to put solvent on the shaved backs of bunnies? If we don't do this, then why do that? We should only do what we would have our children see.

In order to build and maintain animal death camps, we must stand far outside of the heart of living things. The inability to feel the pain, fear, and suffering of animals is the very disease we think we can cure through animal experimentation. The diseases we might hope to cure through vivisection are, themselves, symptoms of the same disease that causes us not to feel the pain of other living creatures. The disease is soullessness and a callused heart. If we could cure this disease, a myriad of symptoms would disappear overnight!

In view of the fact that more than one million children are neglected and abused in this country every year, that persistent torture and killing exists in almost every country, that billions of people go hungry every day, we can see how hard it is to empathize with the suffering of other human beings. How much harder it is to empathize with the suffering of insects, animals and trees, water and air. We may think they are merely raw materials for our pleasure and convenience, which we may use or discard as we wish. But we must develop empathy for all living things.

A reporter on CBS's *60 Minutes* said this about atrocities in Algeria: "Whole families had their throats cut, men and women were decapitated, babies were tossed into ovens and burned alive, pregnant women were cut open and their fetuses ripped out, and their tiny throats were slit too."

Nothing can be said in the presence of suffering except compassion. Nothing can be said in the presence of pain except kindness. Nothing can be said in the presence of fear except love. These are the only acceptable responses. We cannot hide behind national interests, political partisanship, economic advantage, or even such laws as those which allow state-sponsored murder. When leaders know this, they will be able to stop what must be stopped. Leaders will know that to inflict pain and suffering, to pollute and defile, to terrorize, torture, and murder is an expression of a single disease: soullessness.

The awakened soul is the great miracle of life. The awakened soul is the great healer. The awakened soul does not cause pain and suffering. The awakened soul does not destroy. The awakened soul is the lover and the protector of all living things. The awakened soul is the cure for the disease of soullessness.

Leaders are awakened souls.

We cannot legislate kindness, compassion, and love. The legislation must come from the inside, as a direct experience of what life is. We must become a part of the sacredness of life by living in our souls. Our soul is the soul of all, the soul of the world. Our soul knows only one move, one answer, one response, one way: love. Leaders are the embodiment of this love within the soul, and they have only one strategy, one goal, one purpose, one method, one plan: to love and care for all living things.

Leaders will know that all things are living and sentient, and they will act accordingly.

For Personal Reflection

Do you feel that human beings have a right of dominion over other creatures and nature? If so, how did you develop this idea? To what degree do you act in disregard of the sanctity of other living creatures, especially in your work life? Are there ways in which you can live so as to become more mindful of the right to life of all creatures?

20

Pond, Rock, Ripple

We should be very thankful to the planet Jupiter, whose great size and mass produce a gravitational force so strong that wanton asteroids and meteoroids are sucked into Jupiter's big mouth, like dust mites into a vacuum cleaner. Jupiter protects Earth from harm by neutralizing all of these potential catastrophes. We are dependent upon Jupiter, although most of us don't know this.

When we open to reality, we understand that everything is related and dependent upon everything else. Nothing lives an independent existence, although we rarely act in accord with this simple fact. Through meditation, self-inquiry, spiritual practice, and mystical insight, the boundaries of our hallucinated separate existence dissolve. We discover that we drink from the same well, we eat from the same table, we breathe the same air, we experience the same joy or pain, love or fear, peace or anger as all else in creation.

More than 250 million years ago, there was only one landmass, one continent, on the Earth. On that one continent it was easy to recognize that all things were related. There was no "here" or "over there." Whenever something happened here, it was felt there.

We still live on that one original continent. There are not seven continents. There is one, and the fate of each is determined by the other. On that one, we are all connected. There are not four oceans. There is one. There are not scores of territorial airspaces. There is only one airspace. There are not myriad seas and lakes and streams. There is only one. There are not innumerable forests and mountains and deserts. There is only one. There are not many races and religions and nationalities. There is only one. Beneath the appearance of difference, there is sameness. Beneath the appearance of multiplicity, there is oneness. Beneath the appearance of separation, there is connected-ness. Everything we think, say, and do is a rock thrown into the pond of our common existence. Whatever ripples are created by our thoughts, words, and actions wash over all of us, equally. We don't readily see this, because we rarely leave the gated community of ego-istic living, which tells us we are different, separate, and unconnected, one from the other.

Within the sanctum of deep meditation, all differences dissolve. There is only one essence, one consciousness, one heart, one soul. Behind the facade of multiplicity and differences, all things are related, connected, and mutually dependent.

This mystical insight of interdependence has crucial and pragmatic implications.

Every thought, word, and action is an energetic impulse that moves outward from us in subtler and subtler rippling rings of effect. Unless we are able and willing to see what these effects are, we will continually be victimized by our own shortsightedness. We will wonder at the muddi-ness of our common well's drinking water. Who did this? Of course, *we* did, but we won't know it. No one would knowingly pour toxic waste upstream when they know their water supply is downstream. The only way we would do this is if we couldn't recognize the connection between upstream and downstream, between here and there, between you and me.

When driving, we don't keep our eyes locked on the road just in front of the hood of our car. We look farther out and down the road. We look from side to side, and even behind us. We need to take in the whole field in which we drive. We have to have a holistic awareness that includes ourselves, other drivers, the weather conditions, the speed limit, and police hiding behind bushes. We have to be aware of the gas gauge, tire pressure, and the oil light. We have to know where we are in relation to where we are going. We have to notice the road signs and freeway exits. We have to be aware of many things in order to drive safely. We have to take all the information from this holistic perspective, evaluate it, and act accordingly if we are to have a pleasant trip and arrive safely at our destination. We have to be aware of everything we do.

The fact that there are more than 40,000 motor vehicle deaths per year in this country makes me wonder if we have the requisite awareness to drive properly.

I also wonder if we have the requisite awareness to live properly. Americans consume eight million barrels of motor and aviation gasoline and gasohol per day, which contributes heavily to urban pollution and which is harmful to all living things. Do we know the full story behind this consumption of the 15 gallons of gas I put in my tank every couple of days? Do we know how this gasoline is made? Where does the oil come from, who profits, and who is exploited? What is the cost to our common existence of such consumption? If we don't know the answers to these and other questions, how can we make intelligent choices? If we don't make intelligent, life-affirming choices, aren't we just the sorry victims of our own shortsightedness?

We cannot tear down a forest over there for our wood over here. That forest is in our own backyard. We cannot spoil lands and seas over there for our needs over here. The stench of that spoil over there is about to wash up onto the front porch of our house over here. We cannot condone an embargo of Iraqi oil which results in the death of 5,000 Iraqi children per month, simply because we think those children are not our children, that they belong to someone over there. Whenever we hear someone say that tearing, spoiling, and killing over there is in our interests over here, know that person to be a dark and dangerous force of ignorance and delusion.

Leaders must have direct experience of this immutable fact of life: all things are related and interdependent. Leaders will not toss rocks recklessly into the pond of our common existence. They will not be able to do this, once the cataracts have been removed from their eyes. Leaders will be restrained enough in the face of massive profit to question deeply the effects of their actions, and to honestly assess the consequences to our one continent of all that they do.

Leaders will live within the context of interdependence. They will live with the knowledge and feeling of the sentience and sanctity of all living things. Leaders will know how to drive our social and business agendas with the holistic view that is required for safe living. Unless we live from the experienced fact of our interdependence with all of Earth's living creatures and systems, we will not know how to live with wisdom. Leaders will be wise enough to say, "No more dumping upstream!"

Another example of the upstream/downstream relationship is discussed in *Diet for a New America*. Author John Robbins reports that in Costa Rica, El Salvador, Guatemala, Honduras, Nicaragua, and Panama, priceless tropical rain forests are being cleared in order to provide pastures for cattle. The Meat Importers Council reports that almost all of this meat ends up as fast-food restaurant hamburgers. Robbins says that in 1960, when the U.S. first began to import beef, Central America had over 130,000 square miles of virgin rain forest, which accounted for a substantial percentage of the earth's oxygen supplies. In 1985, less than 80,000 square miles remain. At this rate, the entire tropical rain forests of Central America will be gone within 40 years.

Are we enough aware of our interdependence to connect the upstream "I'll have three cheeseburgers" with the downstream destruction of rain forests?

What is the relationship between television and the mental, emotional, and spiritual well-being of our children? Over 35 million TV sets were sold in 1997, with 98% of all households having at least one TV set. There are over 10,500 basic and pay cable TV systems. The 1995-96 average of household TV usage per day was seven hours and seven minutes. In 1996, children between two and five years of age watched an average of 23 hours and 21 minutes of television per week, or about three and a half hours per day. Children between 6 and eleven years of age watched an average of 19 hours and 59 minutes per week, which is more than two and three-quarters hours per day.

Do we or the leaders of television manufacturing and sales companies question the effect of this?

Karl Forsyth, who serves on the board of the Aurora Waldorf-Inspired School in Anchorage, Alaska, wrote the following insightful article about this connection:

Television has become the most pervasive and influential medium in the world today, yet there is abundant evidence that the personal and social costs of our TV habit are far greater than the benefits. Our culture is TV-saturated, and no longer has the luxury of objectivity on this issue. Still, one can observe in recent history where the first-time introduction of TV into aboriginal cultures was quickly followed by a breakdown in the rituals, activities and thought-processes that evolved over thousands of years, resulting in lethargy, cynicism, social alienation, alcoholism, drug abuse, broken families, suicide, etc.

This is not a coincidence, and if one understands the effect television has on the human psyche, it is not surprising. Our collective and individual imaginations have been supplanted by a relentless and mind-numbing video display. If our future well-being depends on creative people that can draw on a wellspring of inner strength, and I suggest it does, then this loss could be the greatest tragedy of the 20th century.

There are many problems with television, but the most serious are related to the neurological havoc it wreaks in children. It is a drug in every sense of the word, inducing a drowsy semi-hypnotic state of consciousness that kills the creative and thinking processes. For children, this means the impulse for (and the possibility of) creative free play cannot exist while they are watching TV. Yet, the most profound and influential neurological development of a person's life occurs in early childhood during creative free play—literally the future of that child (and of our society) is being formed.

As responsible adults, do we not want each child to fully develop their innate creative, emotional, intellectual and physical capacities? Of course we do. They are a crucial part of the child's development, enabling the young child to work with others, to problem-solve, to picture, to envision, to see inwardly, and respond creatively and positively to life's challenges. These innate capacities develop in the early years during creative, free imaginative play. Yet, we unwittingly overwhelm and crush this delicate impulse by exposing our children to the constant bombardment of powerful video images. Overwhelming the child's innate imagination in this way results in a reduced and simplified imagination, which in turn reduces and simplifies the development of their neurological pathways, resulting in an actual "dumbing down" of the child.

Our schools are having to deal with a steady supply of 'damaged goods' - in very large part because of extended television watching. The drug-like and damaging effects of the video media are systemic—they cannot be mitigated by "children's programming." Letting our children watch "children's shows" on TV and video is like giving them a vodka martini in a Batman cup. And since the video media kills the young child's impulse for creative free-play, they adopt a passive relationship to the world—outer stimulation and inner emptiness—which makes them at risk for drug and alcohol addiction.

Any systematic and persistent undermining of the critical development processes of a child results in a crippled adult, in some way or other. This systematic crippling process is criminal, because it robs the child-then-adult of potential they may have had at birth, but now will never realize. The worse the assault on the child's full natural development, the greater the tragedy—not just for the child, but for the society that must now compensate in a host of ways for this loss of potential.

For adults, television is just another drug that we should be free to use or not (although it is in our best interest to weigh the hazards). But our children are another matter entirely. We protect our children from a host of "adult" activities: driving, sex, alcohol, gambling, etc. This is as it should be. But we have a gigantic blind spot when it comes to television, which is so much more damaging to children in the long term, that all the other protections we afford are like rearranging the deck chairs on the Titanic. There is something wrong with this picture!

Joseph Chilton Pearce, an expert on human intelligence, creativity and learning, reinforces Mr. Forsyth's view. In his book *Evolution's End*, Mr. Pearce draws upon 20 years of research to show how TV impedes vital neurological development in children. He writes, "As our damaged children grow up and become the parents and teachers, damage will be the norm, the way of life. We will habituate to damage. Nothing else will be known. How can you miss something you can't even recognize, something you never had?"

The following editorial by Jennifer D. Mitchell appeared in the January/February 1998 issue of *World Watch Magazine,* and is another example of the interdependence of all things on our one continent:

If golf wasn't already the world's fastest growing sport, it is now, after the emergence last year of Tiger Woods—a young, charismatic African-Asian-American golfer who won the renowned Masters tournament in 1997. As a result of his rise to fame (heralded by several sponsorships from big names such as Nike), the golf industry is experiencing an increase in the number of participants from New York to Bangkok.

Although Tiger Woods' name—like his profession—may evoke images of wildlife and fields of green, the impact of the growing golf industry is far from environmentally friendly. In effect, wildlife refuges and golf courses are as dissimilar as virgin forests and tree farms—the later being sterile, artificial environments where natural ecosystems and all of their complexities have been compromised.

While Tiger Woods has been able to move mountains as far as racial and demographic barriers are concerned (minorities, women, and children are now the fastest growing segments of the golfing population), his rise is also quite literally moving mountains. In some cases, golf-course developers have lopped 200 feet off a mountain, and moved up to seven million cubic yards of earth—altering, not preserving, natural watersheds. And because the average course requires a minimum of 50 hectares, subsistence farmers, indigenous peoples, and other groups are being pushed off their lands. Each course also requires heavy infusions of pesticides and fertilizers, along with about 3,000 cubic meters of water per day—enough for thousands of city residents. Residents could soon begin to feel the consequences in water-short areas such as Thailand or California.

The president of the U.S. National Golf Foundation has been ecstatic at the possibility that Woods could attract a million new golfers—and their money—to the sport. But to keep up with this surge in new golfers, some 400 golf courses would have to be built in the United States each year. And the new star's agent told Business Week that he "can make a much bigger impact in the Pacific Rim than he has in the U.S." Yet there are already 25 million golfers and 15,930 golf courses in the United States, and another 25 million golfers and only 4,300 courses in the Pacific Rim—where water is scarce, and land is even scarcer.

Much as in Tiger Woods' sudden rise to fame, many of these Asian Tiger economies have ridden an economic boom. Their financial suc-

cess, however, may prove to be short-lived—an impressive economic surge built on an unsustainable foundation. Similarly, as Tiger Woods drives a new generation toward the sport, golf will increasingly push beyond its sustainable limits. The growing number of golf courses in Asia is already reason for much distress—a symptom perhaps, of the haphazard approach to development that has characterized the region's economies in general. Woods now has the opportunity to help rethink the future of his industry: as the number of golf courses and those lining up to use them grows, the time has come to promote "green" alternatives to traditional greens.

Thoughts and beliefs are self-justifying. We may think and believe that we have the right to do whatever we want. We will always be able to rationalize anything we choose to do, despite any evidence which contradicts our rationale. If we live within the limited context of our ego-identities, we will have no moral, ethical, or spiritual compass to show us the more enlightened path to safe, sane, and harmonious living.

Within the sanctum of deep meditation we find such a compass, which reminds us of our interdependence. We discover that many of our desires are exaggerated expressions of soullessness. We discover that we cannot do whatever we want. We discover that there are universal laws we must obey, within which we must live and work, with which we must cooperate willingly and happily.

If we can reach the sanctum of silence, we will discover a wholeness of being, and within this wholeness of being we will discover a peace and contentment. Being peaceful and content, our eyes will open to see how every thought, word, and action is a rock thrown into the pond of our common existence.

Leaders will have this compass of silence in their hands at all times.

For Personal Reflection

Do you regularly reflect on how what you do affects things at a distance? Do you live your life with disregard or in consideration of the implications of your choices on the pond of our common existence? To what extent do you, in your work life, take the time and care to evaluate the full range of effects your activities produce? Have you ever knowingly disregarded information about negative consequences to people's health and well-being for the sake of profit?

21

Don Quixote

Don Quixote is the main character in a novel written in the seventeenth century by Miguel de Cervantes. Don Quixote loses his wits from reading too many romances and comes to believe that he is a knight destined to revive the golden age of chivalry. A tall, gaunt man in armor, he has many comical adventures with his fat squire, Sancho Panza. Don Quixote's inability to distinguish reality from the delusional projections of his imagination finally leads him to attack a windmill, thinking it is a giant. The giant lives inside his head, although he sees it outside himself, in the world, as the world. Don Quixote doesn't know that his inside is his outside. He thinks the outside has an independent reality. It's easy for us to see his mistake. But we don't see our own mistake.

We too tilt at windmills of delusion, because we don't see how the outside flows from the inside. We don't see how the outside world is a picture, a living replica, of our internal pictures. The world is the topography of our mental realm of thoughts, emotions, beliefs, assumptions, opinions, identities, fears, desires, and denials. Only when we find our way back to pure awareness will we stop seeing the world as we imagine it is, and begin seeing the world as it actually is.

Why does the world lurch from one sad encounter to another? It is only because we think the external world has an independent reality from our internal consciousness. We think that things *just happen,* or we might say that they happen because of someone else, or because of a recession, or because it is someone's policy. We think there are giants when there are only windmills. In order to see the world as it is, we must first recognize the projected world of our delusions and dismantle them.

One of my clients became Don Quixote in a meeting, tilting his outrage at a giant where no giant existed. I had worked with him for more than a year, and I knew his background and his hot buttons. He had been nicknamed "Captain Blast-off" by his team, in tribute to his tendency to launch into reactivity—an unconscious behavior precipitated by unresolved past emotional experiences—whenever his will was thwarted. I had even bought him a toy rocket ship, which he courageously put on his desk to remind him that reactivity, as a state of mind, is the antithesis of awareness.

In this meeting, he was trying to sell his team on a particular approach to resolving a manufacturing problem. No one was responding. They didn't believe his data, his analysis, or his recommendations. They questioned and challenged him. I could tell that Captain Blast-off was about to blast off. I deliberated whether to intervene before or after the launch, and decided to wait until after.

He launched. He started screaming at his main antagonist, the manufacturing divisional vice president, shrieking the man's name over and over in front of the team. Within seconds, he was halfway to the moon.

But here is the strange part. The name he was screaming was the name of a former colleague with whom he had had such battles more than 20 years ago. The president of a company, with tremendous authority and power to influence the lives of many people, had lost complete touch with present time and began jousting with an ancient foe. In that meeting, in that room, at that time, he was Don Quixote, charging at the foes inside his own head. The colleague whose name he was shouting was nowhere to be seen, and had not been seen for 20 years.

Once, a great samurai warrior sought out a Zen master to ask him about a deeper truth than he had ever known, deeper than all his attainments, all his victories, all his renown. He finally came upon the reclusive teacher, and said, "I have heard you know great truths, and I want to know how I can enter the realm of truth, the realm of paradise."

The teacher looked at him scornfully, and said, "You? You want to know truth? You seem to me to be a very stupid and arrogant man, who couldn't possibly understand anything other than violence and killing and brute force."

At that, the famous warrior became incensed and drew his sword to cut off the teacher's head.

"That," said the teacher, pointing to the sword flashing forth from the scabbard, "is hell."

The words penetrated to the heart of the samurai, and in an instant of realization, he put the sword back into its sheath.

"And that," said the teacher, "is paradise."

By evoking these kinds of confrontations with the beliefs of our internal reality into consciousness for scrutiny, we make possible a fuller and richer experience of our potential to see how things happen and why.

Are we aware of the thoughts, images, and beliefs which we project outside ourselves, mistaking them for reality?

I've read several studies which establish the number of thoughts we think in a day as 60,000, although the actual number may be greater.

Every 1.44 seconds, we have a thought, which may include such emotions as anger, frustration, happiness, sadness, jealousy, and disappointment. Both thoughts and emotions belong to the mental realm, and these explosive fireworks detonate within us every 1.44 seconds.

How many of these thoughts are we aware of? How many do we notice? How many do we ponder before we act? How many do we question to determine their validity and relevance? How many do we track back to their origin? Until we become acutely aware of each thought and familiar with the place from which they arise, we are victims of our own unconscious reactivity. We can be neither intelligent nor effective, neither creative nor inventive. We will not be able to see what is in front of us.

Imagine driving along Highway 5 in central California, going 75 miles an hour. Every 1.44 seconds your windshield cleaners spurt oil on your windshield. How can you see the road? How can you ever see what is actually there in front of you? This is what happens in us: a darkening and obscuring oil spurt goes off every 1.44 seconds. We cannot see through the oil spurts to where the real world is waiting. We act blindly and stupidly, at the mercy and effect of a process we aren't even aware of.

Our external world is a direct expression of our internal world of thoughts, ideas, and beliefs. In order to transform society, we must first transform ourselves. We must each first investigate our own hearts and minds. We must each discover how we create and project the very things we want to change in the world. The power of awareness will transform our lives, our institutions and organizations, and society at large. This direct experience of our spiritual consciousness, free from distortions and conditioning, will show us how to live, working with and from values that affirm life in a sacred and meaningful way.

We must see that the crises in the outer world will never be solved until the crisis in our own consciousness is resolved. The qualities of our awareness express themselves as our belief systems, which in turn produce our priorities, our values and goals, our attitudes and behavior. We must face directly the attitudes and policies that have fragmented human and ecological relationships. We must seek deeply within our own hearts for a new vision of compassionate life. The true leaders are those who stand on the frontiers of the spiritual world, shedding the veils of ignorance in order to see that our difficulties are rooted in the poverty of our awareness.

When the philosopher J. Krishnamurti said "the crisis is in our consciousness, not in the world," he alerted all of us to the origin of our actions and the cause of our calamities. If our consciousness is rooted in the fear that shadows a belief in our separateness, then all the world becomes a battleground of self-preservation. If, however, our consciousness is rooted in the mystic perspective of oneness, our motives will be liberated from fear and we will find that we have been immersed in this consciousness from the beginning. Having seen this, having recollected and become conscious of what life truly is, we will then begin to articulate new patterns for action, based on the direct perception of the spiritual reality of which we are a part. This articulation is the province of leaders, whose soothing words steady the dangerously rocking boat of our mind's reckless desires and fears.

We almost automatically attribute our experience of reality to external causes. It is difficult, almost impossible, to recognize that both our experience and our reactions are internally generated and have nothing whatsoever to do with external causes.

What precedes thought? Of what are beliefs made, and how are they formed? What is awareness? What is the mind? What is beyond the mind? Where do reactions come from? These are questions for leaders.

If we are ever to live with insight and clarity, we must ask these questions. But we cannot answer them with intellectual answers. We must follow the trail of these questions to their source. We must put on our hiking boots and fill our backpack with food and water. We must find the trailhead and then walk into the wilderness with courage and resolve. Each of us must become an intrepid explorer. Each of us must face our own obstacles and adversity. We must develop strength along the way. We must become attentive. We must become transformed by the journey itself.

Leaders must take this journey into the wilderness of self-exploration. They must come to know what is within them, the shapes and forms of their conditioned barriers to the radiance of soul. Leaders must exemplify clarity and freedom, and so they must begin to follow the trail of their own experience and reaction to the very source. They must begin now and not stop until they reach the heat of the first fire.

Behind the stream of images and concepts is the field of pure awareness, the uncluttered mind, from which we can see how things happen and why. But when we see and release images and beliefs, it is sometimes painful, as though we die, just a little. We are confronting little tremors of death every time we look at ourselves. Death is but the dissolution of false images of self and the barriers of self-protection we build around them. This process of seeing beneath the surface images of self and our beliefs about the world yields powerful gifts: a clear perspective on the origins of things as they appear in our human world, psychological insights about our personal nature and motivations, the untangling of confusing and dense emotional states, and revelations of universal proportions—transpersonal glimpses into pure awareness.

Study your own self, not through ideas, philosophies and opinions, not through what you already know, but directly, without images and protection. To study oneself is to examine, to inquire without motive, to see without flinching, how one actually lives, thinks and relates. This requires that the deepest parts of ourselves be drawn out into view. When we have come fully out of hiding, we become vulnerable, and this vulnerability reveals the truth of who we are.

The immense task of leadership is to wake up and know which way is north and which way south, to become clear and balanced, to quiet the thunderclouds of anger and fear, to awaken from the slumber of ideas and posturing, into the authentic clarity of the real.

This is the work of leaders.

For Personal Reflection

Try the following practice for one month. Every day, spend ten minutes sitting in a quiet place where you will not be disturbed. Sit comfortably on a chair or on a cushion on the ground. Find an easy posture, with back erect. Allow your attention to focus on your breathing. With every in-breath count one, then two . . . until you reach ten. Then start over. If you lose your place because your attention has wandered, start over at one. At the end of ten minutes, write for another two minutes in a journal. Let your first, uncensored words of reflection come directly to the page.

At the end of the month, write a one-page summary of what you have learned and read it to your family or selected colleagues at work.

22

Dojos and Zendos

In the winter of 1969, I cinched up my aikido *gi* for the first time, bowed, and stepped onto the mat in a small *dojo,* practice hall, in Arcata, California, a little town on the northern coast. The *sensei,* teacher, was a big burly man who looked like a meat packer or longshoreman. Instead, he was a psychologist by profession, and a man of very gentle disposition, although he could throw my ass across the room while barely touching me.

The aikido *sensei* was also the local Zen master, and I had been sitting *zazen,* meditation, with him and a small group of students for a few months. I had already had one of the defining moments of my life with him in *dokusan,* a conversation or interview with the teacher, one that continues to reverberate even now as I type these words. During meditation, the *sensei* would sit in a small anteroom adjacent to the *zendo,* the meditation room, and await any student who wanted to come and speak with him about meditation practice, or anything, for that matter. In the first week of sitting, I decided to go to *dokusan.* I walked in, turned to close the door, and then sat down on the cushion in front of the *sensei.* I looked him in the face across the two feet of space which separated us.

"*Sensei*, I wanted to speak with you about *zazen*. I have been study-ing at the college and know something of Zen and meditation…"

He leaned forward, just about an inch or two, and asked, "What exactly do you know?"

If he'd fired a cannonball from his mouth, I could not have been hit harder. His question exploded and shredded my face with its clarity. I had never experienced anything like that. I honestly think he had no strategy in his question. He just asked a simple question with such pres-ence and clarity that I was incinerated from the blast. It was my first experience with someone who had awakened from the tranquilizing effect of thought overload. The power was enormous. It was as though I had suddenly seen how foolish it was to try and measure the Earth's cir-cumference with a 12-inch ruler. What I thought I knew, and the means by which I knew it, lay in ruins and rubble at my feet.

I remained speechless for a time. I couldn't find my faculties. I had been stunned into silence by a single question. I stared into his face, which was an abyss of patience waiting for my answer. I had none. I got up, walked shakily out the door and back to my cushion. My nascent interest in truth, freedom, and clarity was solidified in *dokusan*. I wanted what he had.

Many of the meditators also practiced aikido with *sensei,* as a way of grounding or integrating meditation experiences and insights into action, into the everyday world. I watched one session and was immedi-ately impressed with the dance-like fluidity of the movements and the general good humor of the participants toward their art. I signed up.

When watching an adept, aikido may look easy, almost staged. There is whirling and turning and flying and smiling. A video of Morihei Ueshiba, the founder of modern aikido, shows him repelling a number of advanced students as they attacked him en masse. All he seemed to do was turn slightly this way or that, maybe duck or twist his hips, maybe extend his arms one way or another. No one touched him. They all just flew through the air and into each other. It looked too simple to be real. I thought that aikido was more of a meditation practice than a useful martial art like karate or kung fu, and that all the attackers were in some covert way cooperating with the elderly teacher. After all, Ueshiba had said, "The secret of aikido is to harmonize ourselves with the movement of the universe and bring ourselves into accord with the universe itself.

He who has gained the secret of aikido has the universe in himself and can say, 'I am the universe.'"

Soon another cannon shot disabused me of *that* idea. During the first session, I tried my hardest to punch a senior student in the mouth. The student disappeared and I went flying. Time after time. Amazing. When it was my turn to be attacked, my awkwardness was stupendous. Had it not been for the compassion of the senior students, I would have been mauled, and probably killed. I was so out of sync with the flowing currents the senior students seemed to move in. I was frustrated and impatient, but also inspired. I persevered, not willing to let my clumsiness defeat me. Everyone kept smiling. *Don't worry, keep practicing.*

During each aikido practice, the *sensei* would work his way around the room to interact with each student at least two or three times. His hands were like ham hocks, except I could hardly feel them when he threw me. I would feel a little pressure, a force of some kind, and then I'd be flying. The odd thing was that whenever the *sensei* threw me, I'd get up smiling. I think it was a combination of his skill and of his demonstration of the founder's words, "There is no discord in love. There is no enemy of love." *Sensei* was demonstrating his love for me. Being thrown by him was an exciting and joyful experience. I always smiled. Of course, when it was my turn to practice a technique on him, I felt like a child trying to wrestle an elephant to the ground. It wasn't very exciting or joyful.

I persevered, because I wanted some of what he had and I thought that devoting myself to aikido was the way to get it. I developed a fantasy of one day living in a small back room of a *dojo* in which I would teach aikido and meditation. I imagined living in this simple way, deepening my knowledge and oneness with the universe by walking back and forth between my living quarters and my aikido *dojo* and zazen *zendo*. I loved the simplicity of the Zen aesthetic; nothing extra, just the essential thing, the thing in itself. I couldn't wait to get my black belt.

As things turned out, I left Arcata about six months after I started practicing aikido and never again stepped on a mat in earnest. The closest I came to realizing my ambition of being an aikido teacher was in a hepatitis-induced hallucination, about four or five years later, in India. In that hallucination, I saw myself living in a small room behind a small *dojo*. Then I heard a sonic boom of laughter and the picture burst into flames.

Before I left the *dojo,* however, I had one tremendous experience. We had been practicing one of the basic techniques for a number of days. It was a wrist throw, a technique practiced by all aikido students, regardless of how advanced they become. Someone throws a punch to your belly, you step off the line of attack, grasp the attacker's wrist, pivot your hips while taking two steps, and then, bringing your second hand to cover the attacker's hand, extend energy. The attacker is supposed to flip, fly, and land. Then you bring gentle but firm pressure to bear on a wrist lock. They tap out and smile. You smile. Everyone bows. Love prevails.

That's the theory. I never came close, except once, when one evening I threw the *sensei.* He smiled. I smiled. "Very good," he said. The euphoria was incredible, and it wasn't from pride of achievement. It was from directly experiencing the flow of love and harmony that I sensed *sensei* was experiencing. It was indescribable. *WHAT do you know?* Here, lick this and tell me how it tastes!

I learned much in the *zendo* and in the *dojo* during the winter and spring months some 30 years ago as I began the practice of disciplines to cultivate awareness. I began to develop an appreciation for discipline, intensity of effort, surrender, and effortlessness. I saw the arrogance and insufficiency of my thoughts and beliefs. I learned about patience, perseverance, humility, and respect. I learned to pay attention and to appreciate the pain that would always follow when I didn't. I learned about my own ambitions and desires, and about how much I lived in the future. I learned how a smile can signify the entrance to the infinite mystery of oneness. I learned that we have to develop our awareness in order to become truly human. I learned about the power of questions, silence, clarity, and openness.

I did not learn these things as one learns the multiplication tables. I did not master them in such a way as to get an *A* or a *B-* on report card. I only began to learn them. I continue to learn them today, although my *dojos* and *zendos* are different. I continue to learn about what I only began to experience on the meditation cushion and aikido mat a long time ago. Even now, the scar tissue of that cannonball crater shines on my forehead.

A *zendo* is a meditation room, and a *dojo* is a martial arts training hall. Whether we use those terms literally or metaphorically, they both refer to specialized environments meant to cultivate awareness, expand consciousness, and teach us to blend with reality. They are places dedicated to enlightenment. Leaders will need to visit *dojos* and *zendos* on a regular basis. I want to suggest a few that will deepen a leader's contact with reality.

The first *dojo* is meditation. This is an essential *dojo*. Leaders meditate. One potent form of meditation is called *vipassana,* or mindfulness meditation. This and other forms of meditation help us to develop awareness and show us the nature and origin of thought and emotion, of reactivity, of beliefs, of grasping and attachment, fear and desire. Meditation reveals the many dimensions and facets of reality. Meditation unfolds the inner being, opens the heart, and stimulates the indiscriminate flow of love. Meditate every day. Learn to follow the breath into the deep hiding place where it rests, suspended between inhalation and exhalation. There, in the breath's secret lair, is the leader's intelligence.

Silence is another good *dojo.* Leaders should know silence, a state of non-dual awareness which grows through the practice of meditation. That silence will come of its own, over time. Until that silence awakens within, practice the silence of not speaking. Do this one day a week, and do it where you work. I don't care if you are the President of the United States or the CEO of Microsoft. Be quiet one day a week. You will be amazed.

Once a year, participate in a weeklong silent meditation retreat. This will unify and strengthen your practice of meditation and of not speaking so that the silence of meditation will awaken within you.

Fast one day a week, and one week a year, after visiting your health-care practitioner to be sure you have no particular ailments that would be exacerbated by this practice. In addition to giving the body a much needed rest, fasting shows us how compulsive and unconscious our eating habits are. It helps to bring awareness of our diet, our bodies, and emotions that are buried beneath compensatory eating. Fasting also reminds us of the millions of people who live in poverty and go hungry each day.

Visit the wilderness and live in nature. Live silently, openly, and humbly in the deep forests, high mountains, or vast deserts. Meditate and fast in silence while living and walking in the wilderness. Leaders must see that nature is not just lumber for our condos and shopping centers, but is a vast storehouse of wisdom, knowledge, beauty, and life force. Go on a vision quest under the guidance of a Native American shaman. Live in nature until the urge to pollute and destroy it has left you.

Volunteer to work in a hospice. Cradle a dying person in your arms as she passes from this world. While caring for those who are actively dying, we might become intimate with our own death, and in so doing we may learn much about living.

I read a story about a mother who was telling her young daughter about her work as an art teacher. She said, "Mommy goes to teach grown-ups how to paint."

The daughter replied, incredulously, "You mean they forgot how?"

Volunteer as a tutor in an elementary school in your community. Go first to the school whose students are from the poorest, the most disadvantaged families. Do some research and volunteer in those schools in your city which have the highest incidence of drug use and violence. Listen to the students you tutor as much as you talk to them. Let them help you remember what you might have forgotten.

A bumper sticker I noticed three years ago while driving on East Blithedale Avenue in Mill Valley startled me: *The Next Time the Air Force Wants to Buy a Bomber, Ask Them to Hold a Bake Sale. Fund Education!*

If you are an elected official, whether a state representative, governor, or senator, a good *dojo* is the poorest neighborhood in your constituency. For one entire month each year, rent an apartment in the absolutely poorest, most dangerous, drug infested, violently depressed, and terrifying area. Live there. Work from your home. Don't hide in Sacramento or Washington, D. C. We should demand that all elected officials practice in this *dojo*. We should make this dojo a requirement of public service. In this way, leaders might come to know the truth of humility and empathy, not just the words, and act accordingly.

We must all practice the art of leadership; therefore, we must all practice deepening and refining our awareness. We must all make judicious efforts to contact reality. We must keep refining our awareness and opening our hearts: this is the leader's work.

Take a trip to a place where you can swim in the ocean with dolphins. Stay with the dolphins until you are able to understand what they have to say.

Leaders need to visit *dojos* and *zendos* to become impeccably aware. Leaders need to confront what they think they know to see if it is in accord with reality. "The secret of aikido is to harmonize ourselves with the movement of the universe and bring ourselves into accord with the universe itself."

For Personal Reflection

Develop your own list of leadership dojos and zendos, places or activities that will challenge what you think you know about reality. Pick one and participate in that on a regular basis for six months. Do not use excuses to absent yourself from participation and practice in what you have chosen. Keep a journal of your experiences and insights.

23
Justifiable Homicide

Lin-Chi, a great Zen master, once said, "If you meet the Buddha, kill the Buddha." What he means is that any thought, idea, image, or concept of the Buddha is not the Buddha. All images or models of the Buddha must be killed in order for the real and true Buddha to come into existence. Leaders will need to kill their models in order to know reality, just as Lin-Chi said to kill the Buddha in order to become the Buddha.

A model is a map, not the land; a menu, not the meal. Leaders, knowers of reality, cannot depend upon models, because models lag behind reality. Reality is instantaneous, spontaneous, and non-dual. A model is just the opposite: slow, constructed, and dualistic, a map which is painstakingly drawn to approximate Yosemite Valley, the Himalayas, the Siberian steppes, the Sinai desert, or any other place.

Models are produced by the mind. The mind itself is a pattern of perceiving reality. The mind constructs models of reality: it filters, evaluates, categorizes, names, prioritizes, and organizes. The mind cannot know reality directly, only by inference. The mind can only perceive reality in its rearview mirror.

Leaders must know reality directly. Leaders will not show us maps;

they will rub dirt on us. Leaders will not read us menus; they will feed us pecan pie.

Models are a separating membrane between us and reality, obscuring our ability to see. Any model is ultimately antithetical to spiritual insight and true seeing, which is always spontaneous and intuitive, shooting like a meteor across the heaven of our mind, and then disappearing forever in a blazing second. Models are dualistic. They exist within the context of "knower" and "known"—the paradigm is the known, and the person is the knower. The knower and the known must come together in knowing, and that knowing is spontaneous and intuitive. Leaders must sacrifice themselves and their models to that knowing.

Many people speak *about* now, *about* being present, *about* the power of intuition and spontaneity, but they don't speak *from* now while *being* present, intuitive, and spontaneous. They speak from the past, from what they have said before, from what they already know. They show maps and read menus.

If we are going to speak about reality, reality should shoot from us like Fourth of July fireworks, booming and exploding, spewing sparks and geysers of light never before seen, never before heard, surprising and delightfully original.

Why don't we trust knowledge to come spontaneously from the well of perfect knowing? Who wants to carry around huge water tanks in their head? Why do we need to, when anywhere we go there is the well of perfect knowing?

It is more important to see who a leader is than what they know. I would like to see leaders who have been struck by lightning and see their split, smoldering, charred-tree-trunk bodies. Leaders should hurl shattering reality bolts in our direction so that we may become instantly split apart and—amid that smoldering wreckage—discover our freedom and essence.

Leaders are free, spontaneous, and original, just like awareness.

It is easy to become lazy and inattentive once we've developed a model of how life is, once a pattern has settled like dust on our eyes. We can become secure and complacent with this knowing: there is always a sock drawer for the socks, and a t-shirt drawer for the t-shirts. The coats go in the hallway.

How does this knowing come about? How do thoughts grow into beliefs, and beliefs into paradigms? We may need to spend long hours just watching how an experience or a thought becomes a concrete shelter or a gun emplacement on the craggy coastal cliffs of our private country of certainty. Should we be content to sit in front of the stage and be amazed by the light and magic show? Shouldn't we want to go behind the curtain to see who the wizard is?

If we want to meet the maker of birds and birdsongs, we will have to dump our socks and t-shirts onto the ground and smash our dresser drawers.

People would sometimes come up to me after one of my weekly evening seminars to tell me how something I had said made perfect sense and had helped them to connect some dots in their lives, though they could sense that clarity already fading. They always wanted to know how to remember *it*. They wanted to lock their insight into a paradigm so they could continue to see what they had seen.

I told people to forget about remembering. What was important was not what they had seen, but their ability to *see*. Seeing results from emptying oneself of everything, and then throwing away the empty self, so that the moment itself lives through us. Marry the moment, love the moment, become the moment. The moment is always poignant, which is why so many were so affected, and the moment is also fleeting, which is why no one could remember.

I walked into the office of a client, a project director for a construction management company. He had forgotten about our meeting, even though I had flown from San Francisco to Boston at his request.

"Well, anyway, it's a good thing you're here. I feel like my 94-year-old grandfather. Every time I visit him, he looks at me and pleads, 'Just tell me where I am!' That's how I feel. I'm so buried with this project, I don't even know where I am."

He couldn't see anything except the shadows of his own anxiety and confusion. His every action was aimed at these shadows producing only an escalation of the tension and helplessness within his office.

We must all learn to clearly *see* what is actually happening and to be able to discern the difference between what is real and what is imaginary. Most people don't see well, if at all. It's understandable, because we have never learned how.

Anaïs Nin wrote, "We don't see things as they are, we see them as we are." Isn't this true? We usually see only our own thoughts and feelings *about* what we imagine is happening, superimposed on what *actually* is happening.

So how does one see more clearly, more realistically? Our first response is to do something, to learn something new. We can find numerous techniques, strategies, and philosophies in the plethora of self-improvement books, audio- and videotape programs, and seminars currently available. We may be tempted to exchange our current model for a new one, thinking it will help us see better.

In order to see, we must be free from patterns, because a pattern—any pattern—is just another projection of our mind onto what we are trying to see. More shadows, less light.

My response to my client's state—as it is with almost all situations asking for clarity, problems asking for solutions, doubts asking for assurance—was to request that he sit quietly, relax, attend to his breathing and let silence suffuse his whole being. I requested that he not think differently or change anything, but that he become more aware by becoming silent.

Awareness is a direct seeing into the moment, without projection. It is clear insight. Awareness is a light that illuminates all situations, objects, and thoughts. Awareness is the eye that sees things as they are, not as we would like them to be, or hope they are, or imagine they are. When one sees with the eye of awareness, appropriate and correct action arises spontaneously out of the situation itself.

In order to see things as they are, we must develop clear awareness. This means that we do not pile our fantasies onto a situation. In order not to add our distorting projections, we must internally free ourselves from images, opinions, beliefs, and interest in outcomes or results. These are all obstructions to clarity. When we dissolve these internal structures of patterned perceiving, awareness itself remains.

We can only see deeply into the pond of the mind if the sediment of thoughts and images has settled through meditation and silence. When our internal structures of patterned perceiving collapse in silence, awareness itself grows like a lovely lotus above the mud.

The philosopher J. Krishnamurti said, "Silence comes when thought has understood its own beginning, its own nature, and how all thought is never free but always old. To see all this, to see the movement of every thought, to understand it, to be aware of it, is to come to the silence which is meditation."

Awareness itself, not representational models, is the means of seeing, of perceiving, what is happening in reality. Awareness is not distorted by first, second, or third thoughts; or by anxiety, doubt, or self-interest. Awareness does not turn away in denial, does not grab with desire. Awareness is simple, quiet, present. Awareness *means* "what is."

The great sage Ramana Maharshi said, "Effortless and choiceless awareness is our real state." Entering into our real state will always illuminate who we are, where we are, and what we are doing. In this way, we will always know what to do and how to do it. We will not become lost in labyrinths of anxiety, doubt, fear, and confusion. We will not need to act rashly from fear or inelegantly from anxiety and confusion. Awareness itself is an engine of enormous power.

Before he disappeared into the clouds, Lao Tzu wrote, "Knowledge creates doubt, and doubt makes you ravenous for more knowledge. You can't get full eating this way. The wise person dines on something more subtle. He eats the understanding that the named was born from the unnamed, that all being flows from non-being, that the describable world emanates from an indescribable source."

True leaders will be able to see behind the facade of the make-believe world to the real world, the subtle world, the indescribable world. True leaders will embody such simplicity and clarity that all who come near will likewise see, and know.

For Personal Reflection

What memories of past experiences does this chapter trigger? Think of a particular experience you had when your perceiving was not limited by your filters, by language, or by your customary perceptual patterns. What does this experience teach you about the nature of reality? What are the implications of such an experience for you in the workplace?

24

Mentored by Carrots

In Greek mythology, Mentor was the trusted counselor of Odysseus, and the word has come to mean "wise and trusted counselor." This notion of a mentor is described and recommended in many books on management and leadership, and is gaining currency in professional training programs. In professional circles, it is thought to be a good idea to have a mentor to teach one new skills, to refine one's attitudes and behaviors, and to guide one's career, especially as one enters the upper echelons of an organization. There, as one begins to enter the narrowing and competitive world of executive advancement, the mentoring becomes increasingly political.

A mentor is a good thing to have. One of my early mentors taught me something that revolutionized my life: the difference between thought and awareness. My mentor, about whom I'll speak later in this chapter, taught me how to pay attention. As my ability to pay attention deepened, I came into the awareness of things as they are, of life as it is. I learned that without this awareness of things as they are, we are asleep and dreaming. Leadership must be rooted in awareness, not in sleep and dreams.

What I learned is the very essence of mysticism. I learned that thoughts and beliefs, which are cults of like-minded thoughts, obscure reality. Reality itself is between and behind thoughts. I learned that each thought is its own advocate, which is why we can rationalize or justify anything—even the crudest and most horrific behavior—because the thoughts behind the behavior are self-justifying. I learned that conceptual thinking, being self-justifying, cannot admit the consequences of its own actions. It cannot make connections of accountability because it only justifies.

I was reminded of this by an article in *The Los Angeles Times* on February 22, 1998, about pilots aboard the aircraft carrier U.S.S. George Washington and their readiness for an air attack against Iraq. Lt. Reuel Sample, the ship's chaplain, said, "Do they worry about hitting civilians? Yes, they do. But to be perfectly honest, in order for them to get their job done, they need to put that out of their minds. We as Christians strive for peace, but sometimes God uses war to bring about peace."

Does God need to use war to bring about peace? Would God ask anyone to put killing people out of their minds? God has nothing to do with this. Thoughts and beliefs and their actions are self-justifying, especially those concepts with which we sincerely and seriously link our sense of self and ego—those which define who we think we are—such as national or religious affiliation and identity.

Blaise Pascal, the French scientist and philosopher, vivifies this with words written three hundred years ago: "Men never do evil so completely and cheerfully as when they do it from religious conviction."

Living within the abstract identities of the ego, we cannot see what we do; we can only see our justifications. We will justify any behavior that serves our beliefs and our identities. In order to live intelligently and harmoniously with each other and with nature, we have to see the limitations and self-justifying characteristics of thoughts and beliefs. We have to develop a desire for truth, not justification. We have to become hungry for truth, and sick of rationalization.

Loyalty to the ego and its beliefs is the root reason behind tragic behavior by individuals and organizations. It is the cause of corporate greed, pollution, and governmental abuse of power. It is why CIA operatives might traffic in drugs, because their loyalty, their allegiance, is to an idea of patriotism, or some other abstract identity used to justify their behavior. They are not committed to the truth. It is why tobacco industry executives might lie, en masse, to an incredulous American public. Their loyalty is to personal and corporate profitability, not to truth.

Leaders must be loyal to truth.

When a thought, idea, concept, or belief is challenged, threatened, or imperiled, the ego responds as though its own life were being threatened or imperiled. In order to see who we truly are, to be able and willing to be accountable for our actions in the world, we need to die to conceptual thinking and become resurrected in awareness.

We have to be exceedingly mindful about those thoughts and ideas with which we identify because they become a description of our self-image; they become who *we think we are,* while who we actually are is forgotten. The strong trunk of identity upon which grow the branches, leaves, and flowers of lesser identities is obsessive-compulsive egoism, a mental tic that obscures reality. If we cannot see or know reality, we cannot act in accord with it. We take our orders from the willfulness of this mental tic of egoism.

We will defend this trunk of egoism and this tree of identities to the death—to the death—against any and all real or imagined threats and assaults. Our survival becomes the survival of our identities. We will deny, discredit, or destroy everything that threatens the survival of our identities. It can be difficult to recognize and name our identities because they may be so barricaded behind impenetrable walls of emotional and psychological defenses, but we can certainly recognize their affect: anger, arrogance, vanity, and conceit.

We can see the wreckage of this reckless behavior everywhere we care to look. We can, for example, see it in the climatic changes in the Earth's atmosphere as a result of an industrial behemoth whose products feed our extravagant lifestyle and whose waste streams are the unpayable bill.

In the introduction to his book *The Heat Is On: The High-Stakes Battle Over Earth's Threatened Climate,* Ross Gelbspan writes, "The reason that most Americans don't know what is happening to the climate is that the oil and coal industries have spent millions of dollars to persuade them that global warming isn't happening."

Of course, we have to ask if we really want to know. We may not, because knowing what is actually happening might be too threatening to our egoistic ideas for and expectations of a comfortable and convenient lifestyle. We may choose to deny what is happening in the world with the magic wands of anger, arrogance, vanity, and conceit.

The mentor who taught me about awareness was a pile of carrots. I lived for four years in an ashram, a meditation center, in India, during which time I was assigned a variety of chores as part of the daily routine. One day, I was asked to work in the kitchen. All the food was cleaned, cut, and prepared by hand. I was asked to become a vegetable chopper. That is when and how I met my mentor. While I also learned from eggplants and tomatoes and potatoes, the carrot was the superior teacher.

I was shown how to hold the knife, how to stand properly, and how to slice each carrot into precisely angled pieces of a certain thickness. This was important. Each slice had to be according to specification: a precise angle and thickness.

Each morning at about 4:00 a.m., I would go to the kitchen to be mentored by the carrots. Every task in an ashram serves a dual purpose. The first is to do the thing itself, to chop vegetables, to sweep a path, to care for a horse or cow. In this regard, it was a job that you were to do as well as you could. The second purpose of any task in an ashram is to mirror your level of attention, so that you can become more proficient in awareness. This second aspect of any task brings the thing at hand into the realm of meditation. Everything in an ashram is a meditation; each and every instant is a means of increasing awareness. That is any ashram's purpose for being: to increase awareness through direct experience of reality.

In the beginning of one's curriculum of task-as-meditation, the Guru or the work supervisor would become the helper of the task. They would point out when the students were not paying attention. The supervisor of the vegetable choppers would watch me with fierce and unforgiving eyes. If my posture wobbled, she yelled at me. If my grip on the knife weakened, if I looked up and around at others, she scolded me. The worst always came when I stared off into space, hallucinating imaginary events. I'd usually be brought back into the present by a potato thud against my head. The supervisor was supposed to do that. It was her job to help me become aware.

The most ruthless teachers of all, though, were the carrot slices themselves. I had been shown what to do and how to do it. Each slice had to be a certain angle and thickness. Knife thrust after knife thrust, slice after slice, carrot after carrot, day after day, week after week. Each slice just so. I don't know that anyone who ate what we prepared with the carrots was particularly interested in the just so-ness of each slice. That wasn't the point. Becoming aware was the point.

The supervisor's greatest joy was in rummaging through my mounds of slices, looking for one that was not just so. For the first few weeks after I started, this was easy. I rarely, if ever, made a cut just so. After a time, I hit the mark maybe one in three, which would have been a good average in baseball. Not here. Somewhere around carrot number 30,000, I began paying attention. My batting average was up to near .800. My posture, grip, and cutting motion were all solid. I didn't look around. I didn't stare into space. I was right there, about 80% of the time. Better, good even. But not good enough. We were expected to bat a thousand, no excuses.

And why not? We had an unambiguous assignment, raw materials, the tools, the training, and the ability. With nothing missing, what's the problem? What's the variable? *Attention.* It was always—and only—attention. Paying attention. I can now, 25 years later, hear my supervisor screaming and spluttering in my face: *Pay attention! Concentrate! Focus!*

Bat a thousand? Why not? What's in the way? I learned that the only distraction to batting a thousand is the quality of our awareness, the clarity of our attention to now, to what we are doing, to what is happening. Even our technique is a function of awareness. This is the great teaching of my mentor: pay attention.

The carrots also showed me why I couldn't pay attention. I was lost in my thoughts, without even knowing it. This is what compromised and corrupted clear attention every time: being lost in thought without even knowing it.

A visitor once asked a New Yorker how to get to Carnegie Hall. "Practice, practice, practice" was the answer. So it is with becoming aware. We practice awareness by paying attention to what we are doing and noticing what happens within ourselves when we stop paying attention, when we slice the carrots out of spec or when we cut our finger.

What happens is that our attention leaps on the back of a thought and rides off into the sunset, leaving the carrots behind, without our noticing. Just as we have to pay attention to what we are doing on the outside, we have to also pay attention to what we are doing on the inside. We lose our awareness, our capacity to pay attention to what is, when, instead of noticing our thoughts and feelings, we become them. This is when we will cut our finger, or worse. If we are running a billion-dollar multinational company, or leading a country, losing our awareness to rampaging thoughts and strong emotional tides will be disastrous.

As I became more adept at paying attention, I began to bat consistently at around .900. Sometimes, for a few minutes, I could bat 1.000. During one of these hot streaks, the supervisor, try as she might, had to let handfuls of carrot slices pour through her fingers without comment. She looked at me. I looked at her. She was not impressed. I was not proud. It was just so. *Here, cut these carrots at this angle and at this thickness. Fine. Done.*

Through this training, I learned how to pay attention to what I was doing, and I could notice much of what was going on inside my body and mind. I had noticed that awareness was behind and around all of this, even marbled through it. I might still go to sleep, but I was able to notice it, almost immediately. As a result, whatever I was doing, I did well—very well. I had become an artisan in life, just by paying attention. It was a time of lucidity. I suppose this was progress.

Then, something finer happened.

Up to that point, my practice field was the carrot piles in front of me, my task, and my thoughts and feelings. One day, a 20-dollar wall clock expanded the playing field. I had never noticed it before; it was too remote from where I was paying attention. Then I heard it tick and tock, tick and tock. I had never heard it before. Now I did. My practice field just got bigger. Spontaneously, I began to notice more and more, farther and farther afield. I could hear people breathe, feel drawers open silently, sense pots being lifted out of sight. This is when the effort of paying attention— noticing what I was doing and what was happening around and within me—was catalyzed by awareness and exploded into something I had not experienced before except in deep, eyes-closed, seated meditation.

I was suddenly alive and awake in a field of consciousness, in which I had clear focus and perception of what was at hand—including the thoughts being dealt like cards from my mind and the commuter struggles of blood corpuscles in my arteries—and the simultaneous sensual or intuitive perception of a larger field that could include two people speaking 50 yards away, a lizard sunning on a rock an hour's bus ride away, or smoothly curved arcs of glowing celestial blue matter, 20 million billion miles long, drifting orca-like between galaxies in deep space.

In this instant, all conceptual barriers to clear awareness dissolved. In clear awareness, the entirety of creation is within the reach of the open mind.

Paying attention until awareness lifts us out of conceptual thinking is meditation. Meditation is awareness, and awareness enfolds all of life. Leaders must know this.

At first, meditation is a practice that teaches us to focus our attention on a single point, perhaps the breath or a mantra or the space between two thoughts. As we focus, we are amazed to discover how many thoughts we have. We begin to see that the mind is nothing but thoughts about things, and thoughts about thoughts. We can observe the chaos of the mind, racing without order or purpose from one thing to the next, careening from the past to the future while barely touching the present moment. We also see that all of these thoughts are self-centered. Our whole internal experience is qualified by a central thought, the image of "me."

As we continue to focus the mind, we begin to observe our thoughts and feeling states without getting lost in them. We see that these mental/emotional states arise in numberless waves within the mind. That which observes the play of thoughts is not the mind but the awareness from which the mind itself is born. We can see that this awareness is qualitatively different from thinking. It has a depth and silence to it. Gradually, we begin to perceive through this awareness, in silence, without thoughts, images, or symbols. And, as we do, our own sense of self becomes transparent.

Meditation dissolves self-centeredness as it carries us into the silence of pure awareness. In this awareness, our spirit is liberated from conditions.

Our entry into this silence marks the end of meditation as a practice and the beginning of meditation as a state of being. Our chronic restlessness subsides. A different way of seeing and knowing is aroused, becoming a capacity of intuitive perception that is holistic and instantaneous.

In the stillness, we feel a subtle, pervasive presence. When we try to know that presence, it recedes, but it returns as we relax and simply allow it to be. Within this effortless perception we see the animating presence of the creative force pervade all things. This is called *sahaj samadhi,* natural meditation. It is the encounter with our Source. It is who we are, once we have relinquished our smallness, pettiness, and fear. As we relax into awareness, we see that we are the background from which all forms arise. We see this glowing presence as a shimmering light around everything. It is indescribably beautiful, and in the midst of this beauty we fall in love with all things.

Meditation is an ending of ourselves and an opening into the Source, which flows invisibly behind the visible world of forms—a flow of beauty, peace, and love. This Source is the very ground upon which we stand. It is the essence of what we are, though we constantly overlook its shattering simplicity.

Whether we see it nor not, the light of the invisible Source shines within us. If we would just sit quietly by the open window of our heart for a few minutes each day, soon that light would be evident to us, and soon that awakened light would heal, inspire, and enlighten us. We would enter reality, knowingly, and become lovers and servants of this reality.

Leaders are lovers and servants of this reality.

For Personal Reflection

Develop your own list of prospective awareness mentors. You can include people or activities. Undertake a relationship with at least one mentor from your list for a period of six months. Keep a journal of your experiences and insights about the nature of thought, mind, attention, and awareness. Include entries that reflect how your behavior and performance at work are affected by the mentoring.

25

Beyond Peace

I was in Delhi, India, in 1984, when Prime Minister Indira Gandhi was assassinated by members of her own security guard. In the days that followed, I witnessed firsthand the horrors and brutality of inflamed hatred and fear. At night, I would stand on the roof of the ashram and count the fires burning throughout the city. I ventured outside during the day on a couple of occasions despite the martial law forbidding this. The army patrols that roamed the city in trucks and jeeps had orders to shoot anyone on sight without warning. Once I saw a charred body sprawled in a park, one blackened arm lying a few feet from the body. I sat down.

I had seen and felt violence before, in other places and at other times. But there was something so stark about this singular encounter. I sat next to that corpse for a long while, forgetting about the roving army units who would have shot me dead without warning. I sat for a long time.

As I write this chapter, I glance over to a stack of magazines and newspapers and notice the following stories:

Today is the thirtieth anniversary of the incident in My Lai, where some 80 U.S. soldiers spent four hours killing 504 Vietnamese civilians, mostly women and children.

Within a three-month period in 1994, an estimated 800,000 people were killed in Rwanda, as a result of ethnic conflict between Hutus and Tutsis.

The Palestinian security chief warned Jewish settlers that they would "not leave alive" if they tried to attack residents of Hebron's Palestinian-ruled areas again.

The Bosnian-Serb army interned thousands of Moslem and Croatian women in camps where they were gang raped for weeks at a time to demoralize them.

Since the Chinese invaded Tibet in 1949, over one million people have been killed, and over 6,000 monasteries destroyed.

More than 25,000 people, most of whom will be civilians, will step on a land mine this year. According to the Red Cross, almost two million land mines are planted each year in killing fields around the world.

Metin Bakallci, who runs four Human Rights Foundation centers, said reports of torture in Turkey have declined in recent months because the police have developed methods that leave no traces—such as laying the victim on a block of ice before applying electric shocks.

A bomb exploded on a train in Punjab province, killing at least five people and injuring 20.

Is there a single place on this Earth where people are not committing or sponsoring violence, war, repression, and terror, whether militarily, economically, or culturally, overtly or covertly? Is there a single place that has not been desecrated and ravaged, any single square inch of earth that has not been a burial ground? Is there any place where purity and innocence remain?

Let's be honest. The world is a spastic convulsion of violence, and we are that world. We must begin here. We must admit this truth without protest, embarrassment, or equivocation, without blame, defense, or explanation. It is the pure and simple truth. Whatever peace exists is but a facade, behind which is more brutality waiting to break out. We must go beyond such peace.

Peace, as the absence of conflict, violence, or war, may be achieved for a moment, but then that moment turns over and the dark side of peace breaks out, bombastic and vehement. This kind of peace is only a temporary suppression of violence. It may last a day, a year, or a hundred years; yet within this extended moment of peace the vibrating seeds of war are waiting to burst open. We must go beyond peace.

Wars do not end because we have not found the courage to end violence within ourselves. We will stop only when we are willing to see the cause, only when we go beyond peace. Has peace ever been achieved, once and for all? No, it has not, because the peace we say we want, the peace we try and achieve, is not peace at all. It is only a suppression of violence.

Leaders must end violence within themselves and end war in the world.

The Sufi poet Rumi wrote, "A True Human Being is the essence, the original cause. The world and the universe are secondary effects." If we are to find what is beyond peace, we must know who we are beyond our egos, our identities, our masks of secondary effects. We must know our essence, which loves without demand, lives without fear, serves without expectation.

Violence is the by-product of living within our defined identities: *man, woman; Democrat, Republican; white, black; Israeli, Palestinian; Christian, Moslem; Bloods, Crips; holy, sinful; born-again, pagan; heterosexual, homosexual.* Living within these identities, we are always afraid of the other and of that which we are not. Our survival is dependent upon the survival of our identities, and those who are different will always be a threat. Even if peace and harmonious accord are established, fear remains. It is only a matter of time before we are again in conflict with the other. We will always be suspicious, and therefore afraid.

We have to go beyond the peace that is only a truce with violence. We have to return to the original cause, within which is a peace that cannot be disturbed.

This peace which cannot be disturbed is waiting, just on the other side of nearby doors. One door is love. One door emanates beauty. One door opens a millisecond before death. Another door hangs poised between two thoughts, and another door rests like a harbor seal on the flat shiny rock of the breath as it pauses between in and out. There are many doors to that which is beyond peace.

Why then, if we want peace, do we not open these doors to our essence?

Leaders will live within the unbreakable silence of their essence. Leaders must go immediately through the doors to that which is beyond peace and war, beyond conflict and fear, beyond violence and ignorance. There is our home, there is our essence, there is our truth.

Leaders must know their essence. This is the way to end violence and hatred in the world. Leaders must have the courage to demonstrate this knowledge, and so to inspire it in others. Leaders must know how to meet another on the ground of original cause, original being, original essence. Leaders must meet others without fear, without desire, without identity.

Leaders must meet others in the spirit of that which is beyond peace.

For Personal Reflection

Make a list of ten identities that define you. Who are you without these identities? How would you act if you let all identities go? Can you do this? Have you ever experienced yourself without identifying with anything? What was that like?

26

How to Change the World

Even though the truth of our being is present and revealed within us at all times, we do not usually experience this truth, know this truth, or speak this truth. We have to first work to get at it, and then we have to work to live in it. After a while, living in the essential truth becomes natural, and we couldn't leave that truth, even if we wanted to. It does take work and practice to find, experience, and speak this truth of universal mystical essence. Until we do, we have to say that we are liars about life because if we do not tell the truth, then we tell lies. To tell the truth of who we are is difficult, though we must—all of us—now begin to do so. Certainly, leaders will have to do so, or they cannot be leaders.

Just as it is difficult to speak the inner truth, so is it difficult to speak the outer truth, to represent explicitly and precisely how we act and what we do—without anything else added. Just the bare presentation of facts, no extraneous adjectives or adverbs, only nouns and verbs: actions and items. *I threw this rock through that window.*

There is a strong correlation between being able to speak the truth of our inner being and being able to speak the truth of our outer actions. Both are essential. Both are hallmarks of leaders.

Telling the outer truth of our actions is difficult because, though we are told as children to tell the truth, most of us get into trouble when we tell the truth.

"Did you take those cookies from the cookie jar?"

"Yes."

SMACK.

We won't again admit that we took any cookies, not if it means getting hit on the head. We'll say, "No, I didn't. I swear I didn't. I think Rick did."

We often make others uncomfortable when we speak the truth. We often elicit disapproval, or worse: *Do you have to say that? Why can't you be nice? Don't rock the boat. You're being disloyal. Let's just put that behind us. It's not nice to hurt someone's feelings. Don't rat on your friends. You should be ashamed of what you did.*

We quickly learn that telling the truth is risky business, so we learn how to obscure and spin the truth for approval, security, acceptance, to get what we want, or to avoid punishment. We condition ourselves to instantly distort the true facts of our lives, so much so that we aren't able to know, within ourselves, what is true about our own motives, desires, and actions. The truth is terrifying to us.

In the late 1980s, I led a series of seminars in San Francisco, New York, and Boston. On the morning of the second day of a two-day seminar in Boston, we sat together in a truth circle. I asked everyone to consider saying something that they had never told anyone before, something they had kept secret and hidden from view.

The rationale for this exercise is simple: if we want to transform ourselves, to free ourselves from falsehood, to liberate ourselves from anxiety and fear and conditioning, to experience truth, then we will have to tell the truth. We will have to put our *actual* lives on the line. All transformation begins from where we are, by admitting what is true, what is actual, about our lives. This might be painful at first, but telling the truth will ultimately bring exquisite health, joy, and radiance to our lives: the truth will set us free.

The ground rule was that participation was voluntary. I was only offering the opportunity to explore the power of truth-telling. One's story need not be about what one did, or didn't do, but could be about anything they had kept hidden and secret. One has to just get used to telling the truth of things that have actually happened. From this, we can grow toward full and immediate accountability and disclosure of our own conduct.

In the first go-around, people admitted fairly benign things. *I stole a bag of candy when I was seven. I cheated on a math test. I blamed the broken vase on my brother. I lied on a job application.*

It was a beginning, albeit a modest one. I asked people how they felt when they spoke these previously unuttered truths. They felt relieved and somehow strengthened. I asked people how they felt about the others who had spoken these truths. They said they felt empathy. No one felt criticized, threatened, or judged.

Then I asked people to have another turn. I asked them to rummage through their boxes of forbidden experiences and bring one out. I reminded them to just say what happened and not add explanations or excuses. People reported truths that were a bit more revealing. The practice of the first round resulted in more significant tales. After this second round, we could feel a definite shift in awareness; we had come to a more acute state of attention. A new force, like a weather front, was gathering within each of us. A small truth had led to a larger truth. Truth was catching hold. I asked people if they wanted to have a third try, and they said yes. They almost demanded it. They were ready, eager, anxious, to purge themselves of congestion, inhibitions, and long-held fear and shame.

This time, people said dramatic and explosive things. *My father made me suck his penis every day for ten years, from the time I was five. One night last week, I ate a large jar of peanut butter, two bags of Oreo cookies, and a one-pound bag of M&Ms and then made myself vomit; I've been doing things like that all my life. My father got so mad at me once that he killed my cat in front of me and nailed it to my bedroom wall. I masturbated with a crucifix and when I came I screamed Jesus' name. I stole about $25,000 worth of equipment from my employer and sold it in flea markets. I watched an elderly woman being beaten and robbed in a subway and did nothing to help her; I walked off the platform.*

Telling the truth requires practice. We have to learn how to get in touch with our inner and outer truths, and then we have to become fearless enough to speak those truths. This is the only way we will find out that truth has the power to liberate, enliven, and empower—and to free us from fear, shame, guilt, and delusion. This is the only way we can discover that we need not fear truth, that we can live and prosper in truth. Truth is a cleansing and purifying drink whose potency restores vitality, health, and radiance to our lives. Telling the truth is hard and often terrifying. Sometimes we don't want to face what we actually do. We'd rather deny what we did or find a way to pin the tail on someone else's donkey, because we may feel that the truth is too shameful. Alcohol and drug co-dependency, familial dysfunctions, sexual abuse, corporate and governmental fraud and corruption, police and military brutality—all of these exist as a function of secrecy, fear, intimidation, and shame. We often repress the truth of our actions and the actions of others through a personal code of denial, thinking this denial absolves us of responsibility and protects us from consequences.

Most of us also subscribe to another kind of self-protective code, a club code like the Mafia's code of *omerta,* silence. These codes are meant to protect people within a particular group from the inquiries of outsiders. Codes of self-protective silence prohibit truth and accountability, ensuring the group's survival. Almost every corporation, organization, institution, and bureaucracy—secular and religious—have a code of omerta every bit as insulating as the Mafia's.

People who break codes of silence and speak out on behalf of truth and accountability are often demonized, vilified, persecuted, imprisoned, even killed. These truth-tellers and boat-rockers are branded by others as heretics, pagans, traitors, and whistle-blowers and are routinely condemned.

Jeffrey Wigand is one such example. The vice president for research and development with Brown & Williamson Tobacco Corp. between 1989 and 1993, he began to tell the truth about the tobacco industry. It, in turn, embarked on a campaign to discredit him, personally and professionally, and to sue him for violating the terms of his confidentiality agreement. It was made to seem that the larger crime was to reveal the truth, rather than what the truth revealed.

That's the way it usually works, although there appears to be a real outbreak of truth-telling and whistle-blowing going on in the world today. Whistle-blowers are very close to being saints. I would love to see a thousand saints of conscience wake up tomorrow and call a thousand press conferences.

Telling the truth is risky business. It is tricky business too, because we each see the world differently. The various factors and conditions of our subjectivity—past experiences, self-image, race, national and religious affiliation, gender, language, mental acuity, emotional maturity, and so on—make it almost impossible to agree upon a consensus truth for anything. I am always interested in the feedback I receive after a seminar or talk. After one memorable evening of lively dialogue with a group, I was told that I was articulate, inspiring, powerful, arrogant, condescending, too mental, full of bullshit, witty, humorless, intense, and not intense enough.

It is also difficult to come to a common sense of truth because our thoughts and beliefs are self-justifying. Any strong thought or feeling we have about someone or something tends to define our truth. If someone hurts our feelings, cheats us, betrays a confidence, or does not return our love, we can quickly create a truth that is merely a function of our emotional reactivity.

Let me illustrate what I mean by *telling the truth.* In 1990, I moved from Mill Valley to Austin, Texas. I loaded up my rented U-Haul truck and drove away, following the route I had plotted using a map from the local auto club. After two days of driving, I got to Austin. The map had told the truth. If I had followed the map's route and ended up in Nashville, the map would have lied.

Can someone follow the directions of our words and get to the truth of our actions, or would they end up in New Orleans?

Leaders must be maps of unerring precision. It is difficult, but not impossible.

We have to start telling the truth, whether or not we want to be leaders. You and I must step forward and show the hand that threw the rock. The poet Robert Frost said that "anything more than the truth would be too much." We are in the habit of saying much too much, spinning spun truths, hardly ever speaking the actual truth.

On November 5, 1996, USA Today *reported the results of a study conducted at RAND and the Harvard School of Public Health that revealed the full extent of medical negligence in the U. S. The annual toll of medical harm includes: 1.3 million injuries, 180,000 deaths, and total costs of $50 billion.*

There is a very practical reason for telling the truth. Telling the truth makes what is real, real. A lie distorts the simple fact of our actions and is composed, in varying measure, of fantasy, denial, belief, rhetoric, dogma, fear, guilt, shame, greed, anger, rationalization, and justification. Relative to actual events, a lie is unreal, and the truth is real, and nothing is more practical than reality.

When we speak lies, we create an unreal world, an abstract world. If our lies have force and conviction, which they usually do, we end up believing them ourselves. We then live in this unreal, abstract world. We grow up in this world. We go to school in this world. We work in this world. We try to solve problems in this world. We marry and have children in this world. We pray and worship in this world. We grow old and die in this world. The celluloid world of movies is more real than this unreal world of our lies.

It is hard to tell the truth; still, we must enter the actual world of how we are and of what we do. If we don't, how will we ever be able to change what needs to be changed, to fix what is broken, to soothe what hurts, to find love in a joyous world? We must start telling the truth, the whole truth—not just the distorted truth, the partial truth, the half truth, the truth that makes us look good by deflecting culpability, or sells our product, or wins that contract, or gets us elected. The whole truth. Anything less is a lie.

When we tell the truth, the real world appears. When the real world appears, it is not as terrifying as we imagined it would be. We can begin to work with what is, in the real world. As painful as the truth circles were, everyone felt a tremendous relief after telling their truths, after admitting to themselves and to others that something was so. It really is no big deal. What is a big deal, what is a terrible deal, is the false, unreal, abstract world of lies. It is like living in hell. It is hell. It is the weirdest failure of all.

For the sixth year in a row, the U.S. maintained its lead as the world's major exporter of bombs, tanks, and jet fighters.

Telling the truth is synonymous with leadership. To tell the truth, one must know the truth, and to know the truth, one must seek the truth. Seeking, knowing, and telling the simple truth is the sum total of a leader's work.

If we don't do this, this world, which was made as a paradise, will become an unendurable hell.

Tell the truth.

Tell the truth.

Tell the truth.

We have to get very serious about this, very unforgiving of leadership liars. We must absolutely expect and demand the truth. We cannot turn away from this. We've got to plug in our bullshit meters, and when the needle hits red, we have to speak up. Loudly. Persistently. We must learn to live in the real world.

We must categorically demand truth and accountability from our leaders, and we cannot allow them to hide behind any shields. We have become much too complacent. We barely yawn when political or corporate leaders blow more smoke and soot out of their mouths than Mt. Vesuvius when it covered Pompeii.

We have come to expect it. This is a tragedy.

To become more aware, more conscious, and more friendly with reality requires that we make the covert overt. It requires that we reveal secrets. It requires truth and accountability. Every person in every corporation, organization, institution, or bureaucracy could help the cause of reality by telling the truth.

Indulge this fantasy:

Yes, my company manufactures, markets, and sells cigarettes. This product kills a half a million people in America each year—and two and a half million more per year around the world—inflicts untold suffering on millions of others, and costs America as much as $100 billion dollars a year. In the past, this company has tried to boost nicotine's potency to more easily addict smokers, and this company has studied ways to attract the attention of children so they would want to buy our product. This company has woven a 40-year tapestry of lies, deceit, corruption, and greed. Ranking members of this company have lied under oath to Congress, the American people, and the world.

The truth is a powerful force. Telling the truth is the first step; accountability—ownership of actions—is the second. Accountability opens the way for penance, healing, forgiveness, change, and transformation. Telling the truth automatically reveals accountability. The fantasy continues:

In telling the truth, I have to admit that it was I, not a company, who has been making and selling this deadly product. In telling the truth, I am able to see the consequences of my own actions. I cannot hide any longer. I can no longer hide what I know; I can no longer argue that people should be free to buy what they want to buy. The simple truth is that I should not make such a product, which is far deadlier than crack cocaine and heroin. If I continue, I am a brother of the Colombian drug lords. Are my fields of tobacco less a killing field than the world's cocoa plant and opium poppy fields? Having told the truth, I can see all of this now, and it is terrible. I don't know what I was thinking. As of this moment, I will stop. I will find another way to make a living and support my family. Now that I have told the truth, now that I have seen the reality of what I have done, I cannot do this any longer.

Telling the truth means we know what we are doing. Being accountable means that we know who's doing it. When we know what we are doing and who's doing it, we can then change and transform, but not before. Truth, accountability, and transformation: this is the holy trinity which will save us from ourselves.

This world is our world. Whatever exists in our world exists because we have created it. Once we accept this, we can change what we want to change. We have the power to re-create our creation. But we have to tell the truth and be accountable.

In a recent television discussion between the Reverend Jerry Falwell and Larry Flynt, publisher of *Hustler Magazine,* Flynt said, "I am a businessman. My magazine is a reflection of what people want. It does not represent what I want. I just give people what they want."

I don't object to Flynt's comment on ethical, moral, or aesthetic grounds. I do, however, object to his statement on the grounds of accountability, or rather the lack of it. "Giving people what they want" is a marketing commandment. It is also the very summit of unaccountability.

"I'm just doing my job" is another summit in the mountain range of this foolishness. "I was just doing my job" could be called the Nuremberg defense. It is ludicrous. Leaders will never say, "I'm just giving people what they want" or "I'm just doing my job" because they have too much respect for truth and accountability.

Leaders understand that if we can first bring the actual world forward, we can then bring the real world forward. Let's become a nation of whistle-blowing, boat-rocking renegades, soaked in truth-telling and drenched in accountability. Let us do so for love of freedom, truth, and reality, with respect, love, and compassion. This is a voluntary exercise. It is not another excuse for witch-hunts and burnings. This is not an opportunity to cast out another's demons for the sake of our own fear, anger, guilt, or shame. We tell the truth here, inside ourselves, in our own home. We say, *Yes, I threw this rock through that window;* or we say, *No, I did not throw this rock through that window.* Both statements must be a map that will get us to Austin.

Let's bring the actual world forward, and then the real world. Let's bring our actual selves forward, and then our real selves. Let us find out whether or not the truth will set us free and, if it does, then let's learn how to live freely, in joy, in love, and in truth. Leaders will live in truth and accountability, setting themselves free and inspiring us to experience that same freedom.

If we cannot tell the truth about how we live, we will never be able to show the truth about who we are. They go hand in hand.

For Personal Reflection

Ask someone you trust to be your partner in a truth-telling exercise. See if you are willing to tell them what you have never told anyone. What does it feel like? What are the barriers to telling the truth of how you live, of what you do? Have you ever participated in something at work which required you to distort or disguise your actions? Why? How did that feel? What do you think would have happened if you had told the truth? Was the trade-off worth it?

27

The Creative Power

On the first day of any client's individual retreat, I schedule each person for an extended session of body work with a masseuse. Massage is wonderful. Its effect relaxes the body, stills the mind, and liberates the spirit. It is the perfect entree to meditation, and meditation is the perfect entree to awareness and contact with reality.

One particular client told me he had never been massaged. With some trepidation, he agreed to it. I brought in my top gun, an associate who was not only an extraordinary masseuse, but also a highly skilled intuitive. I had come to value the insights about other clients she discerned from their physical bodies as well as their subtle energy bodies. She would often see images, symbolic of the client's beliefs or of repressed prior events, which proved to be accurate and useful.

She came upstairs to my office after her first session with this client, collapsed into a chair, and sighed. She was exhausted.

"What happened to you?" I asked.

"I'm going to raise my rates," she joked. "I've never, ever, not in the hundreds of people I've worked with, ever experienced anyone so closed. He is not made of flesh, but of concrete. There is no life force moving in him; his body is almost dead. All his energy is in his head. He can only

think. He can't feel his emotions or his body. I kept getting images of
fear and shame: I think he's terrified of his body, embarrassed by it, and
has closed off to physical pleasure. He's totally guilty about sex. Does he
get angry a lot?"

"Yes. People never know when he's going to go off."

"Too bad he doesn't get off. His anger is really his fear of himself, of
his own body and his sexuality."

Does it seem inappropriate to speak about sex in a book that pur-
ports to be about transcendent leadership? It isn't, especially in this
book. Leadership is an accord with reality, with the cosmos, with the primal life force, with that rapture of being which exists beyond the fear-
based atmosphere of ego identities.

The mystical experience is, in a manner of speaking, orgasmic. It is
deeply blissful, peaceful, energizing, unifying, and ecstatic. The mystical
life is a deepening of intimacy and friendship with reality, and mystics
become the love-force within the life force. Mystics become sensitized to
subtleties of perception, sensation, and feeling. Their bodies are not
transcended but transmuted: from concrete to stamen, from fear to love,
from shame to joy.

Back in their heyday, the Monty Python comedy troupe wrote a skit
in which one of the characters responded to the question "What are your
hobbies?" with, "Strangling animals, golf, and masturbation." The BBC
censors would not permit the word masturbation on British television.
The skit was aired, but with the offensive word deleted.

It was, apparently, inoffensive to strangle animals, but offensive to
touch one's own body in a pleasurable manner. We in America are every
bit as uptight and fearful of sex as the British censors. There is tremendous ambivalence towards sexuality in our culture, and it is certainly
something for leaders to become aware of and resolve within themselves.

We are entranced by sex and sexual imagery, by eroticism, and at the
same time we condemn and vilify our own delight and interest. On the
one hand, sexual imagery is the mainstay of corporate advertising. Sex
and nudity are sure ways to guarantee box office receipts and are the
cornerstone of most TV tabloid and talk shows. Revelations of the sexual
orientation of celebrities will make magazines fly off the stands, and stories of politicians' sexual shenanigans will make headlines for months,
as we know too well.

Adult services, books, magazines, videos, and merchandise are a multi-billion dollar industry. On the other hand, we prohibit ourselves from speaking openly about sex, our children from learning about it, our teachers from teaching it. Is it any wonder that it took Ronald Reagan years to even say the word *AIDS?*

We would sooner speak of strangling animals than sex.

Sexual energy is creative energy. It is the energy of life itself—the ecstatic creative impulse of primordial consciousness. As we try to regulate and repress it through fear, shame, and guilt, we become estranged from that very force which created us, the world, and the universe. We become afraid of intimacy with the very cause of our existence. This is a supremely weird failure of self-betrayal.

We should not be afraid of sex, or the organs of sex, because penises and vaginas are everywhere. Every living thing is born of sex. Sex is everywhere, as strong and heady and dizzying as crushed gardenias. Each cell of each living thing is sexual in its own way. Even stars are born through the stupendous sexual encounters of forces, male and female, copulating to the music of God.

When we repress our life force, it can only be expressed in twisted, angry, and shameful ways. If we allow what is natural to come out from its underground hiding places, we will see that we do not need to be afraid of sex, sexuality, eroticism, pleasure, bodily ecstasy, or intimacy and love.

We secretly long for our bodies to sing, but publicly we get angry at sex and at sexual people and sexual things. We forbid intimacy with certain parts of the body, though we dream of it.

Really, the problem is not with sex, the problem is with our guilt and shame about sex, and our fear of surrendering to the creative pulse and vibration of reality. Fear, shame, and guilt—not sex—are our problems. These create the distorting torque of natural sexual expression.

If we cannot love this creative source of life, we cannot love life. If we repress the sexual energy, we suppress life, creativity, joy, and love. If we control and regulate our bodies because we are afraid of joy and pleasure, we will become angry, and our anger will lash out at others, whose bodies are also our body, at animals, whose bodies are also our body, and at the world, whose body is also our body.

If we cannot love the sacred pleasures and transcendent beauty of our own body, if we cannot sink our separate body into another's and thus find the single body of our true being, if we cannot fearlessly love and be loved, pleasure and be pleasured, then how will we ever love reality? How will we ever delight in this world? How will we ever know communion with another?

Leaders will not be afraid of sex. They will love the very creative power which created them. They will worship this energy, dissolve in this energy, and flood the world with this energy.

An interesting subculture is emerging in America: sexual healers. These are women and men who have studied the ancient sexual/spiritual path toward mystical union with reality. Leaders might want to study in the dojos of these healers and teachers of sacred sexuality. They can show us how to release our fear, guilt, and shame about our bodies, how to befriend sexual energy, and how to blend with the creative power. We must learn to delight in the eroticism of life. We must become skillful and articulate about sex, eroticism, and pleasure. We must speak openly of these things.

Many people in our society have renounced the unquenchably ecstatic nature of physical reality in the name of one belief or another, or of fear, shame, or guilt. Leaders will need to announce, not renounce, the ecstatic nature of physical living.

Leaders should visit the temples of sexual healing and learn from their priestesses and priests. Leaders will consecrate their own bodies to joyous and ecstatic living. Leaders must learn to touch everything with the hand of a lover seeking only to give pleasure and love. Through sacred loving the soul becomes the body, the spirit becomes the flesh, the world becomes heaven.

For Personal Reflection

What are your beliefs about sex and its proper place in one's life? Where did you learn these? Do you feel you have any shame, guilt, or fear about your body, about sexuality, or about speaking about sexuality? Do you see the connections between sexual energy and creative energy, physical vitality, and joy in life? Do you and your spouse/mate/significant other speak openly and candidly about sex and sexual desire? If you feel inhibited about sexuality, are you willing to explore ways to become free?

28
Eating Eternity

On a warm summer day in Santa Barbara, California, I had lunch with eternity.

I was a participant with about 20 others in a meeting whose purpose was to inquire into truth. The meeting was led by Jean Klein, an elderly Belgian teacher of non-dualism. We were sitting in folding chairs or cross-legged on the carpeted floor or on the couch that had been moved to the back of the large living room. Jean was perhaps 80 years old at the time, white-haired and translucent, the embodiment of silence. He was like a waterfall of pure acceptance. Standing beneath his spray, I breathed with lungs I didn't know I had.

He would say a few words and then fall silent. Someone might venture a question. He would respond. Then more silence. We passed the morning like that. His speaking was itself a form of silence, each word coming slowly, with precision, from a deep well. You could almost hear his mind falling like an empty pail into an invisible depth, filling, and then being drawn up by his careful voice.

We stopped at about noon, and went outside for lunch. I sat with Jean and a few others at a picnic table. We ate slowly, silently, still appreciating the atmosphere of the morning. It seemed to me that we were all attentive, mindful of what we were saying and doing, respectful of others, listening with our entire bodies to the total environment. It was natural, without technique or effort. It was simply a condition that had been established of its own accord.

We ate ice cream for dessert. Then, as we sat together on the benches, with our elbows and forearms collapsed on the tabletop, the world dissolved. I took a breath, and it was my last.

There is perception, but no perceiver! There is perception, but no perceived! All worry is worry about me and my body; I'm just an idea and not really worth worrying about. Love is this . . . no other . . . nothing other . . . only this wholeness . . .

Everything I've ever thought is just ridiculous. My God, we should all just sit down and shut up and not move—that would really be the best thing.

What are these electrical flashes and currents? This is all energy! Pure energy, vibrating and singing!

I simply disappeared, but remained present, as an awareness. I looked up and saw the sky and the clouds, but the seeing was with eyes that were not mine. I looked at the others, and saw myself. Everything was bright and radiant. It was so simple and so awesome. There were cognitions, but they were too fine for words and passed quickly, as a silent commentary on the pure feeling of just being, everywhere at once.

It seemed that everything was alive in a way I had never noticed. The grass of the lawn, the dirt clumps at the base of a lemon tree, its bark; at the end of the bench was a woman whose hair shone; the air itself—all this was alive, breathing, growing, moving in *something,* a kind of force, a comforting presence. When I looked at something, it looked back. There was no separation, no difference. I did not own this seeing; it was not mine, not my eyes.

A cognition that came several times was *how beautiful, how beautiful.* I thought of all I had read and studied and learned, all I had experienced. Then I laughed. I thought of the worries and fears and hopes with which I was often concerned. Then I laughed. I thought of myself. Then I laughed. It was pure laughter, joyous as never before, not because of anything, but in and of itself. Who was thinking? I don't know. Who was laughing? I don't know. There was no solid center, no place I could call "me." Like salt in water, I lost my granular self.

It was the most marvelous calamity, the most terrific loss: a falling away of self, all in an instant. I knew, without knowing, this creation is alive and conscious. This creation is beautiful; this creation is beheld silently, in wonder and awe. A conscious presence lives at the center of all things, underneath all things, within all things. There is an order to life that is out of time. It is eternal, but fully present and revealed in each moment, in each thing. The silence grew deeper and the loss more total.

There was just pure existence. If there was thought or movement, if there was discussion and laughter, it happened by itself, to no one in particular. Things seemed far off because they happened to no one, but everything glowed brightly, clearly, so full of *itself,* the presence.

So much was lost, and so much gained. It was so apparent, how did I miss it? Here, now, in this very minute, as we are, seated at a picnic table, eating ice cream, is depth upon depth of loveliness and silent beauty. *My God, how much I love this creation that I am!*

There is so much order, intelligence, and fullness in the creation that we are. There is so much beauty, so much love, so much tenderness. This is what reality is. We find ourselves in this loss of self, in the opening to mystery, in seeing the luminous presence that brightens all things.

I would say that we must realize this, but it is already realized. I would say that we must return to this seeing and knowing, but we have never left. I would say that we must find this within ourselves, but it exists equally without. I can only affirm that we are this silent beauty, that we do live as the living presence in all things, that we are love.

I want to hear leaders speak of this. I want decisions to be made in the light of this reality. I want the silence of eternity to be the foremost advisor of leaders everywhere.

If leaders will serve eternity, the world will sleep well.

For Personal Reflection

Rewrite this chapter, using an experience you've had in place of the one I describe, an experience that connected you to the transcendent world to which I refer. To what extent does such an experience influence your work life?

29

A Spectacle of Silence

I once witnessed a spectacle of silence in the Berkeley Community Theater. Every one of the 3,491 seats was occupied. On stage sat Thich Nhat Hanh, a Vietnamese Buddhist monk. Next to him sat a young woman. The monk spoke about mindfulness, about awareness, about respect for each other and all living things. He spoke slowly and quietly. From time to time he would fall silent, and the woman would pick up and ring a bell that rested on the floor in front of her. The reverberations of the bell could be heard throughout the auditorium and felt within each person's brain, stimulating perceptions of intuitive subtlety.

Thich Nhat Hanh's talk was less about information than about experience. The words were like a tour bus, carrying the audience to ancient sites of meaning and depth and beauty. Though the bus was still and unmoving, we traveled far and saw much. Anyone could have dropped a tack or a nail file, even a piece of paper, and the noise would have seemed loud because the silence was so great.

After some time, I felt the audience breathe in unison, a meditative breathing, a breathing that connected us to each other and to the awareness of which the monk was speaking. I thought I was sitting in the mountains at twilight, when life itself begins to creep from its hiding places like a deer come to drink from a lake of pentagrams and stars.

Even when speaking, the monk was silent—was silence. In order to hear his words of silence and the silence within his words, the audience had to be silent and become silence. It was a spectacle. We were embraced by silence and thus set free from agitation, separation, and duality. It would have been impossible for any anger or cruelty to arise in that community. It would have been impossible for anyone to harm another in any way. We were transported to reality.

The world needs this silence. Leaders, like the monk, will be of this silence. Their minds will be silent, their actions will be silent, their hearts will be silent.

Silence cannot be explained. It cannot be known or experienced in a way that might be familiar to us, or as we are used to experiencing other events in our life. However, when we say *beauty* or *love,* and when we are meeting those two in a pure and honest place, then we can say that silence has come into our life.

We can only use words to point in the direction of silence, such that if one actually goes into the distance toward which the words point, one will eventually come upon silence as a fact. When silence is beheld as a fact, all speculation, argument, and belief about that to which the word silence refers ends—instantly and forever.

Silence is that in which everything exists, from which everything comes, and into which everything returns. It is the unutterable context in which the cosmos occurs, a playground of pure consciousness.

Silence is oneness. Silence refers to a state of fundamental unified existence, a condition of *being* in which all conflict, fear, doubt, projection, memory, and delusions—all subjectivity and objectivity—are dissolved, and thus resolved. Silence is an instantaneous recognition of that which is out of time and unconditioned by cause and effect. If one were a religious person, one could say that silence is the soul of God, or perhaps the God of God.

If this sounds abstract, vague, or esoteric, it only sounds so because we cannot say exactly what silence is. Some things are so very beyond the reach of words and metaphors, symbols and images, beliefs and concepts that all attempts to describe them are foolish. And yet, even as we speak foolishly and impertinently of that which cannot be said, something within us will smile knowingly. It is this intuitive resonance which words can stimulate. This is the direction we can point to and go toward, walking or running, in order for the recognition of the wordless to become real. But even as silence becomes indomitably real, as taut, tense, and thrilling as a tidal wave crashing upon us, crushing us beyond recognition—even as this happens, we cannot speak its truth.

Any disciplined practice that involves focusing the mind will eventually lead to silence. Spiritual methods such as meditation techniques, chanting mantras, yoga, tai chi—all of these will lead to silence. Self-inquiry will lead to silence. So will martial arts, dance, and art. So will rock climbing and sky-diving. So will cooking and eating. So will playing and loving. Everything will lead to silence, because silence is the life force behind everything. It is the oxygen without which everything would fall over dead, flash frozen. Since all things lead to silence, we must follow the echoes of silence, inward, to the source of all things within us.

Being led to silence might imply that silence is somewhere else. This is only a figure of speech. Silence is always the first thing and the last thing. It is always present, but very subtle, so we must learn to recognize it. The direction of silence is any direction. There is no place that silence is not, although we cannot apprehend it with our senses or with our minds.

Still, let me suggest a foolproof way of coming into silence quickly, so that silence becomes a fact for us. First, we must develop the ability to distinguish one thought from another. When we can do this, we must then develop the ability to clearly see the space between two thoughts. When that space becomes large and stable enough for us to drive a truck through, we will know silence as a fact.

In the very center of universal manifestation, one finds swirling gusts of silence, vast galactic streamers millions of light years long. If we try to understand this silence through our mind, we'll never understand it. Silence is realized in a moment of communion, in a moment of losing our separation from life. The underlying truth of existence is silence.

Silence embraces everything and cannot be known because to know silence, we would have to be separate from silence, and silence would then be an object of our perception and of our knowing. Silence refers to that which is beyond this dualism of knower and known. Silence becomes a fact when we and life become an inseparable whole. Even though we are trying to define it, no definition of silence is accurate. We don't want to think that by defining it, we can know it. Silence is knowable only to itself, and we come into that knowing through an alchemy of self-transcendence.

We can only create a definition that points to silence. The truth of reality is silent. It is undisturbed. It is causeless. It is out of time, out of space, non-dual. Silence is the preeminent nothingness in which the universe dances in spectacular and mysterious ways.

If silence is the United States, then intuition is Ellis Island, the first stop of immigrants seeking asylum. Intuition is the first hint, the first experience of the far greater country of silence. Intuition is not a tool, but an intelligence that uses us. We might not see this right away. Intuition is willing to be used, but only for a time. One day, it will require that we suspend our goals and objectives, our plans and aspirations, for a fuller recognition of what intuition is, what it represents. We will come to see that intuition is the ambassador of silence, and we must serve that silence, for it is the soul of the world.

In the instant of intuitive perception, we are taken wholly into that power of knowing which is beyond the mind. In going beyond the mind, we go beyond all notions of self and identity, of thought and belief, of perceiver and perceived. A photograph of the intuitive flash would show only light. There would be no other image, only light. The light of intuition is the light of consciousness. Intuition is Ellis Island, the gateway to freedom. In order to be free, we must want freedom; we must be willing to leave behind the old countries of control and manipulation from which we have come. We cannot come to this new country with ideas of exploitation, as gangsters. We have to come as servants of the new freedom. We have to learn new ways of living. We have to become students of silence and freedom in order to learn how to live without fear, without violence, without cruelty.

The world needs this silence. The world needs leaders who know and serve silence.

For Personal Reflection

What value do you place on silence? What are the ways that silence influences or affects how you make decisions, how you listen to others, how you act under stress? *Consider a one-month experiment: to maintain silence for an hour a day, and for one day a month. Keep a journal of this experiment. At the end of the month, write a five-minute talk summarizing your experiences and what you learned.*

Epilogue:
Whirling Dervishes

To ask leaders to know reality is to ask them to cross a crucible of glowing coals with bare feet. At first look, it seems impossible: the beds of red- and white-hot coals cannot be walked on without incinerating the feet. Reality, just like the other side of the coal bed, might seem too far away, to impossible to cross, to know.

In 1994, I was asked by a client to design a three-day retreat for his company. We established the themes as leadership, customer service, teamwork, and unprecedented levels of performance. This last one was our real focus: how to teach and inspire people to do things they've never done before. The retreat was named "Climbing the Mountain," and was held at Snowbird, Utah, during the summer.

On the second evening we went outside, all 220 of us, and gathered in a large field surrounded by craggy mountain ridges painted with the fading colors of dusk.

We built three pyres of wood, set each on fire, and waited for the structures to collapse into heaps of coals and embers. They knew what was coming; we had spoken about walking across the beds of coals inside.

The group was diverse: men and women from age 19 to 84, all sizes, shapes, and colors, of many different nationalities and religions. Almost all thought they wouldn't be able to walk across the coals.

As we waited, drummers drummed and dancers whirled around the fires.

When the pyres collapsed, we separated into three smaller groups, with the members of each group taking turns raking the coals into 14-foot rectangles. By now it was dark, and the sparks from the glowing beds lifted up into the night like crazy fireflies.

Drummers pounded on the big drumheads, slowly and rhythmically. People stood silently in their groups, waiting to do, to be, the impossible. Who would go first? Would anyone?

Someone yelped, broke from the crowd, and ran across. Cheers and screams rose with the sparks and brightened the sky.

The drummers quickened the beat.

Another cry, another runner. Then another. The drumming boomed.

Two hundred twenty faces shone red in the night. Two hundred twenty people caught the fire of freedom. Another runner, then another, too many to watch at once, too many to count.

One by one, then in twos and sometimes threes—holding hands, cheering, singing, shouting, crying—people ran across, then danced across. Everyone went once, most twice, some wouldn't stop. The drummers' mallets pounded on the drumheads, throwing huge sounds up and against the cliffs. The runners and dancers lived on the coals, walked across, stood for minutes.

Everyone danced and whirled across the fires of impossibility.

In the 13th century, the Persian mystic Jelaluddin Rumi founded a sect of Sufism known as the whirling dervishes. Rumi said, "Let us whirl like a compass around the point of divine grace." One does not need to be a Sufi to be a whirling dervish. The dervish's dance is a universal dance, the dervish's turning is the celebration of life, the dervish's whirl is the elaborate soul of the cosmos.

I have seen Sufis dance in this way, arms outstretched, heads erect, turning and turning, twirling and whirling faster and faster, always precise and perfect, until they abandon their forms for formlessness, until their physical bodies become spiritual bodies, until they leave the visible world and enter the invisible, still dancing, turning and turning, lost and found in love-making of exquisite subtlety, sinking into unfathomable depths of rapture and rising to majestic heights of self-release, spinning and turning, turning and dancing, succumbing again and again to the miracle in which all life turns and dances in freedom, in joy, in love—and then, after hours, maybe days, maybe weeks, the turning and turning gradually slows, the rapture of formlessness becomes the ecstasy of form, the invisible world becomes the visible, the inner becomes the outer: the world becomes the point of divine grace.

The whirling dervish is a gift of the invisible world to the visible world. Our world needs leaders who know how to whirl, who do whirl, and who will teach us all how to whirl.

Our world needs transcendent leaders who are seen only as beauty where beauty is, as kindness where kindness is, as joy where joy is, as truth where truth is, as awareness where awareness is, as life where life is.

Our world needs transcendent leaders whose intoxicating fragrance reminds us of our own, who have visited eternity, who know what death knows.

Our world needs transcendent leaders who live in silence and speak silently. Our world needs leaders who serve our mystic soul, the same one that we all share, the same one that we each are.

Our world needs transcendent leaders whose eyes we trust, whose heart we know, whose soul is rampant in all that they do, seen and unseen, heard and unheard, done and not done. Our world was made to whirl like a compass around the point of divine grace.

Our world needs leaders whose only turning is this turning.

Selected Bibliography

Barks, Coleman (tr.), *The Hand of Poetry: Five Mystic Poets of Persia,* Omega Publications, New Lebanon, N.Y., 1993.

——, *Feeling the Shoulder of the Lion,* Threshold Books, Putney, Vt., 1991.

——, *This Longing: Poetry, Teaching Stories, and Letters of Rumi,* Threshold Books, Putney, Vt., 1988.

Bly, Robert (tr.), *The Kabir Book,* The Seventies Press, 1977.

Brunner, Borgna (ed.), *1998 Information Please Almanac,* Information Please LLC, Boston, 1997.

Chollet, Laurence B., "Seven Years in Tibet," *Shambhala Sun,* September 1997.

Earth Island Journal, San Francisco, Volume 13, Number 1, Winter 1997-98.

Forsyth, Karl, "Television Robs Our Children of Their Potential," Computers in Education web site (http://www.corecom.net/~karlfpp/asd-comp.htm).

Hanh, Thich Nhat, *Being Peace,* Parallax Press, Berkeley, Calif., 1987.

Hatengdi, M. U., and Swami Chetanananda, *Nitya Sutras: The Revelations of Nityananda from the Chidakash Gita,* Rudra Press, Cambridge, Mass., 1985.

Havel, Václav, "The Need for Transcendence in the Postmodern World," Independence Hall, Philadelphia, Pa., 1994, Václav Havel web site (http://www.hrad.cz/president/Havel/speeches/index_uk.html).

Jensen, Carl, *20 Years of Censored News,* Seven Stories Press, New York, 1997.

Krishnamurti, J., *You Are the World,* Harper & Row, New York, 1972.

———, *Freedom From the Known,* Harper & Row, New York, 1969.

Klein, Jean, *I Am,* Third Millennium Publications, Santa Barbara, Calif., 1989.

———, *The Ease of Being,* The Acorn Press, Durham, N.C., 1984.

Mitchell, Jennifer D., "Editorial: The Tigers," *World•Watch,* Washington, D.C., Vol. 11, No. 1, January/February 1998.

Moyne, John, and Coleman Barks (tr.), *Say I Am You,* Maypop, Athens, Ga., 1994.

———, *Unseen Rain: Quatrains of Rumi,* Threshold Books, Putney, Vt., 1986.

Nisargadatta, Sri Maharaj, *I Am That,* The Acorn Press, Durham, N.C., 1982.

Pearce, Joseph Chilton, *Evolution's End: Claiming the Potential of Our Intelligence,* Harper Collins, New York, 1992.

Pine, Red (tr.), *The Zen Teaching of Bodhidharma,* North Point Press, San Francisco, 1989.

Robbins, John, *Diet for a New America,* Stillpoint Publishing, Walpole, N.H., 1987.

Robbins, Tom, "The Meaning of Life," Special Supplement Insert, *Life Magazine,* Vol. 14, No. 16, December 1991.

Russell, Peter, *The Brain Book,* E. P. Dutton, Inc., New York, 1979, pp. 212-213.

Schiller, David, *The Little Zen Companion,* Workman Publishing, New York, 1994.

Smithsonian World: *The Quantum Universe,* Unapix, New York, 1996.

Walker, Brian (tr.), *Hua Hu Ching: The Teachings of Lao Tzu,* Clark City Press, 1992.

The Wall Street Journal Almanac 1998, Ballantine Books, New York, 1997.

White, John (ed.), *What Is Enlightenment?* "Meher Baba and the Quest of Consciousness" by Allan Y. Cohen, Paragon House, St. Paul, Minn., 1995.

Winokur, Jon (ed.), *Zen to Go,* New American Library, New York, 1989.

Woodward, Bob, *The Choice: How Clinton Won,* Simon & Schuster, New York, 1996.

Wright, John W. (ed.), *The New York Times 1998 Almanac,* Penguin Reference, New York, 1997.

About the Author

Robert Rabbin is a contemporary mystic, author, and catalyst for clarity. He began practicing meditation and self-inquiry in 1969, and subsequently spent ten years studying with meditation master Swami Muktananda. Since 1985, Robert has been lecturing and leading Truth Talks throughout the country, as well as mentoring individuals and consulting to corporate executives. He is the author of several books and numerous articles. For contact information and details about Robert's work, please visit his website at www.robrabbin.com.

Hampton Roads Publishing Company

. . . for the evolving human spirit

Hampton Roads Publishing Company
publishes books on a variety of subjects,
including metaphysics, health, integrative medicine,
visionary fiction, and other related topics.

For a copy of our latest catalog, call toll-free
(800) 766-8009, or send your name and address to:

Hampton Roads Publishing Company, Inc.
1125 Stoney Ridge Road
Charlottesville, VA 22902

e-mail: hrpc@hrpub.com
www.hrpub.com